Advance praise for
Saving Myself: A Los An

"Jeanne Simonoff's beautifully written memoir explores what it means to be human, to overcome hardship and loss, and to come into one's own. It's full of life, and we are with her all the way. The book is a complete delight: poignant, charming, brimming over with observation, vitality, and the will to survive." —Kathleen Spivack, poet and Pulitzer Prize nominee, *Moments of Past Happiness, The Beds We Lie In*

"I have been enthralled by this inspiring memoir of a child's experience of profound loss and survival; a story of individual resilience and familial care. This is an intimate glimpse into the mind of a child with irrepressible vitality and strength. Thanks to Jeanne Simonoff for her contribution to the literature of childhood loss and recovery." —Jane Napier, psychotherapist

"Fall into the mind of a little girl. A compelling, funny, sad, and richly written memoir told through a child's perspective about her loss, love, and the rite of passage into adult life and the family, and deep connection to family that carried her there." —Jan Marquart, LCSW, author of *Echoes from The Womb, A Book for Daughters*

"This memoir of discovery and healing leads us to the delightful Queen Stinky, who refuses to take a bath. The author brings the child's voice and the child's strategy to power in this lyric work." —Patricia A. Murphy, Ph.D., author of *Searching for Spring, We Walk the Back of the Tiger*

"In *Saving Myself: A Los Angeles Childhood*, Jeanne Simonoff writes lyrically and passionately so that we can hear the lost who speak 'without voice,' and also vividly evokes the voices of family and childhood, of wonder and terror, against the backdrop of post-WWII anti-Semitic Los Angeles and its layers of history." —Anya Achtenberg, author of *The Stone of Language* and *The Stories of Devil-Girl*

Also by Jeanne Simonoff:

"Walk with Me," *Citadel*

"I Wander through the Streets," *America Sings*

"A Love Poem Starts Like This," "Leaving Home," "A Poem for Gunilla,"
Common Lives

"The Woman Who Is Cello," *West/Word 5*

"Lessons of Sacrifice," *West/Word 6*

"Chocolate," *Eating Our Hearts Out*

"Poem for My Mother, II," *Manzanita Quarterly*

13, A Book of Poems

Credits:
Author photograph by Douglas Gruenau

Visit www.Writeoutpress.com and
www.JeanneSimonoff.com

ISBN: 061538501X
EAN-13: 978-0-615-38501-3

LCCN: 2010902958

Saving Myself:
A Los Angeles Childhood

For Katherine who understands the process

[signature]

A Memoir by Jeanne Simonoff

WRITEOUT PRESS
SANTA FE, NEW MEXICO

Acknowledgments

I would like to acknowledge Natalie Goldberg for giving me a paradigm called Writing Practice, and a community in which to grow my memoir; Kate Braverman for teaching me how to marry my poetry and prose; Eloise Klein Healy and her Los Angeles Writer's Workshop, where the poem *For My Mother Who Died Without Warning* was written (this poem became the hieroglyph for the memoir); David Gardner, my writing buddy and friend, for work-shopping with me through this memoir; Eldorado Writer's Group, Judith and Bonney, who heard early bits and pieces; Pat Murphy, my heart sister, for going the long haul on this process; Anya Achtenberg for working with me through the first few drafts of what became this memoir; Kathleen Spivack, my writing coach, for her help and constant encouragement; and a special thanks to my family, the cast of this book, and my homegrown family, who encouraged me to tell my story.

To the memory of my mothers, Alice Welcher Simonoff and Esther Goldenberg Simonoff, and my father, Robert Leo Simonoff. Their love is unquestionable.

This book is dedicated to all my mothers.

1943

The First Death

E ven though I was there, I can't remember if I caught a glimpse of the flashing red lights or heard the siren when my mother died; whether my father picked me up or I stayed in my crib for what seemed like forever, or just a second. Life after that became a blur. I only remember one small artifact at a time. Sounds: scream, siren, Father's wail, breath, then no breath. Grasping, wife for husband. Beloved, then no beloved.

There is only a mass of tangled feelings, with the Los Angeles summer heat carrying the scent of jasmine in through the open window.

No words; without a map to follow. My father a beacon, then no light.

Only my grandmother and grandfather, Bubbie and Zaydie. Me.

I don't remember what happened the moment the ambulance left with the dead silent body that was my mother. I only have fractured memory. Remembering with pieces missing, not unlike the burning away of a rumpled piece of paper, one that held the story of the leaving. I try to bring order to a place where there was none; I am a small animal lost in the woods. Time, the trickster, plays the game of abandonment.

Dashed, a broken glass, refraction of light cannot connect pieces of the story because of the fissures. Nothing comes forward.

Sometimes I see a movie. The child screams as the mother walks away, held in the arms of someone unknown, screaming until darkness falls.

Why can't I see death like the replay of a film? Gather some understanding by virtue of walking through it at the age of two-and-a-half, with little language? I am small. I leap over the side of my crib, falling to the ground. Then as fast as I can, I run through the bathroom into my mother and father's bedroom. I run to my father. I would have seen her carried out on a gurney toward the front door, as my father holds her limp hand and wails the words, "Alice, Alice, no, please don't go. Please, Alice." Maybe I just stand there trying to grab onto his leg as he pushes me away and leaves me in this house of death.

I don't say goodbye. I don't tell her, "I love you." I don't get a chance to see any more than a body covered by a sheet, and my father going out the front door to see her taken away, if this is what I really see.

I don't get to jump up onto her lap and kiss her goodbye.

There are no words of parting for me. Only screams and cries.

I hold myself. There is no mother. All that is gone. There is only darkness.

I don't go with the sirens. I stand on the front porch. The big red box called "ambulance" goes by. It has a haunting whistle. It sounds like my mother leaving. It is the end and then the beginning.

The Second Leaving

I saw my father walk toward my grandmother's front door. I heard it open and then close. I ran to the window. He got into his car. He drove away.

I remember it was the summer when I was almost three. Summer in Los Angeles, when air is defined by heat and dryness. No sense of rain. No seasons to hint how long it had been without the navigational force of a strong hand to point due north. Longitude and latitude doing a do-si-do dance. One day living with my mother and father, and the next, staying in the house of my grandmother and grandfather, Bubbie and Zaydie.

I was a child who spewed out questions that have accompanied me on the long road from there to here, where I now sit and write. Questions echoed with bull's-eye accuracy. "Where did she go? Did you ever find her? Did you see her? A big jolly woman in a dark gray dress, with glasses, her hair pulled back in a bun? Did you see her?"

No answers. Time seemed to stand still. "How can we get her back? Why did she leave? Was I real bad? Did I wet my pants and she said, 'Not again'? Can I be better?"

My voice rising, pausing, and then shouting out, "Did you kill her? Did you see her leave? What about the baby in her stomach before she went?" I stood shaking, as if a cold wind had caught me in the midst of summer.

I continued on in this litany: "Did you get a letter? Did she leave a note? Did you call her friends? How about Mary Smith? She lived near us. Maybe Mommy told her what I did wrong.

"Did you check her closet? Her red jacket. Did she take her red jacket? That was her favorite. I smiled when she wore that." I remembered my mother and Mary Smith sitting outside, me in my stroller, the two of them giggling about the things they did together when they were young girls.

"How about her books? Were any pictures missing? Like the one with Daddy holding my hand and me holding Mommy's hand?"

Questions went on instant replay day and night.

Now Daddy was gone, too.

Zaydie said he would be back. I needed Daddy and so did Zaydie. Now my questions were about him. "Did I do something really bad and scare Daddy away, too? Did he go with Mommy? Was his car in the driveway?" I remembered running outside and his car wasn't there. I remembered this but I was not there anymore. I was with Bubbie and Zaydie, so I can't be sure that it happened exactly like this. "Did he call work? That's what Mommy would have asked. Did his best friend, Robert, know? Had anyone seen him?"

Questions and peach ice cream, the kind my father said was homemade. We got it after nursery school up at the corner on York Boulevard by Bubbie's. I knew he'd be home pretty soon and then we'd get some. Peach. That was my favorite.

I remember how frightened I was; I thought the worst, that I could have been alone in the house when my mother left, with her voice trailing out to the street, then my father's, too. No one to save me.

Did I kill him? How could he leave right after her?

Bubbie sang those old songs from Russia in the minor key, songs that caused a thunderstorm to fall when she let her tears loose. She began doing that all the time and wove one more word into the lines of the songs: funeral.

Like a mantra plaguing my thoughts: "Bubbie, can we keep the lights on? Does Zaydie know where they are? They should be here right now to take care of me. I am a child. I need them," but Bubbie replied, "Daddy will be back."

Again I begged to go home. I missed my bed. I missed my mother and my father. Bubbie tried to comfort me, "Quiet, my *saena madela*. I'll sing you to sleep."

I dozed off; the waft of jasmine at the window, but there was none. Screams of my mother, but she wasn't there, or was that her breath I heard loud? Slow. Too soft. Then Dad and his cry. Then just me there with Bubbie.

Zaydie went off to work. He'll be back later. Maybe Mommy and Daddy are helping at the store. He'll walk in with them in a little bit.

Bowl of cereal. Soft gray cat. The backyard—a place to hide and look for them everywhere. But I turned up nothing.

Rice pudding. A small wait. The sound of footsteps down the street. I counted them: one two one two one two. Maybe Zaydie is coming. One two one two one. I ran into the street, looking both ways. I didn't hear words except in here where the heart lies. I ran back inside.

"Bubbie, are they coming back? Did I make them go away?"

The phone rang. Bubbie answered it. A lot of words went in and out.

"It's your dad."

I ran to the phone.

My Father's Story

My father didn't know what to do when my mother died. After he buried her, he decided to leave. He was angry that his wife suddenly left. No notice. One minute they were sleeping, but even before the alarm clock went off, she started pulling at him, trying to wake him out of a good dream, a deep sleep.

"She's dying," he shouted.

So he called the ambulance. After it came, he took me to my grandmother's house. Then came back to our old house, and packed two bags, one for me, and one for him, in the suitcases he and my mother saved since their honeymoon. They still had the stubs of train tickets inside. One said "New York City" and the return ticket: Union Station, Los Angeles. He couldn't shake the loss. He didn't think he could raise a child alone. He said he had no choice. He said, "I can't see it ending up another way. Someone else will take care of her." He was sure of that. After all, he came from a family with three sisters and a brother.

"I just have to do this first. Get my head back on straight. Take care of the immediate," my father said.

He stayed with me at Bubbie's until the funeral. I was not allowed to attend.

My father figured I understood.

And so he began the trip to his cousin Emanuel's in San Bernardino before the traffic of people coming home from work was too heavy. He would lose himself in the trail of automobiles. A Chevy, a Pontiac, a Ford. Each one of them holding a stranger, each one having nothing to do with the other. They were all going in one direction, out of the metropolis of Los Angeles with its skyscrapers, into the spread-out farmland, the orange groves. Each driver had his window rolled down. Oranges were in blossom, their fragrance alive and present, like the comfort of a mother's morning song to her small child, as they ate breakfast oranges, sliced open, alive, the juice flowing out. My father saw my mother do this many times. She would take half an orange, place it face down, and pull the handle to move the press that pushed the juice through a small hole into a glass. He saw her now through his tears. He continued to drive the frontage road, numb, staring.

He began to sing a song, the last one he danced with my mother:

"I'll be loving you, always. With a love that's true. Always. Not for just an hour. Not for just a day. Not for just a year but always."

Then fear took over. He was singing only to himself. She was gone.

He steered his car away from the sunset, east toward San Bernardino, toward his future that would hold him, at least until tomorrow.

Bubbie's Stroke

I

Daddy is back. We are living in Bubbie and Zaydie's house. My mother is gone. I am lost.

Bubbie sings *Oyfn Pripetchik,* a special song in Yiddish, and nothing else matters to her.

"Mama, where are you?" It's my father's voice shouting out in the middle of the afternoon.

"I hear her now," Bubbie says.

"Who?" I ask her. "Who?"

The voice she hears is the voice of my dead mother.

Then Bubbie gets off the couch in the living room where we have been sitting. My lunch rests on the table. It looks like it could have been from yesterday or the day before or last year or all the way from the time Bubbie learned the song. It trails off and then she is up and dancing.

"Oh, Mama, there you are," my father says as he comes in the door. "I'm glad you're home. I want to tell you…"

"Wait, Leo, my *kind*; listen to the music, the violin. It's like Uncle Yissel is playing."

"Who, Mama? It's just us here. Just us."

"What's wrong with Bubbie?" I say to my father, frightened. I run to him and grab hold of his leg.

"Let's go," he says, and we walk out the front door.

It's summer and it's hot. It's like no other day before this. My dad and me together again. We walk two blocks up to the ice cream parlor.

"Jeanne, come in and sit down. Let me tell you something."

I remember the fresh peach ice cream. Not my father's tears interlaced with his explanation of Bubbie's loss of reality. It is never mentioned again.

"Peach ice cream." I lick the cone and then hand it to my father to taste. It smells just like the peaches we pick from my Aunt Gertie's tree.

"Good," we both agree.

By the time we get back to Bubbie's, she is in the kitchen.

"Where have you two been?" she says, as if the first act, the song, the dance, is just a dream. Nothing in this waking time can imagine itself into that interlude.

"What's for dinner, Mama?" my father says as he comes in, kisses his mother on the cheek, and proceeds to fetch the silver to set the table.

"*Shabbas*," Bubbie says. "Don't forget. Good dishes."

"But, Mama, it's Tuesday."

"Never mind, you can't trick me. We'll be late for services, so hurry up," she says, discounting that there is anything but her truth.

She goes into her room and lies down. She is quiet and I hear her crying, whimpering.

"Bubbie, what's the matter?" I say to her as I come to the bed by her side.

"Nothing, my *kind*. Come lie down." But I know she is crying over something she has lost. I don't know what, but I know that much.

Bubbie and I take a nap. I still taste the peaches. I still feel the sugar, my tongue tracing the trail of ice cream from the inside of the cone. I am happy. I am three where time slips back and forth like hopscotch and there is no marker to pick up and I am next to my grandmother and she loves me. She holds me to her and I feel safe.

Now, if I am very still, I, too, can hear my uncle's violin. And wherever Bubbie is, so am I. I sleep next to her. It will be *Shabbas* and we will light the candles and in the surprise there comes the *Shabbas* Queen and then Bubbie is happy and then my father is happy and then we all fold down and sleep.

II

I want to ask my father about Bubbie. "Where does she go when she is singing?" My father says Bubbie goes somewhere else but I can see her here, so how can that be?

"Daddy, please tell me how Bubbie goes away."

"She just leaves, but she doesn't leave. It's a grownup thing that you can't understand now. Trust me on that," he says to me.

So I just sit there in the afternoon, on the lawn swing with Bubbie, and wait for Dad to come home from work.

He will be here soon; I know he will.

When he comes home, I say, "Ice cream?" And he says, "Yes."

"What about Bubbie? Can she come, too?"

"No," is all he says. Just no.

We don't talk all the way to the ice cream parlor and when we get there he says to the woman behind the counter, "Two peach ice cream cones, please."

It's the same day in and day out. Bubbie settles back into herself when Dad is there and I go about the day with Bubbie wherever she is and that is just okay with me.

In the singing of the heart, Bubbie is in the soul of what goes and what stays. She is as present as she can be. It is we who are stuck in the day-to-day routine, one thing directly following the next. And who, after all, is to say which is best.

Playing with Bubbie

There's a conch shell on the shelf in my bedroom that Bubbie gave me to hold up to my ear to hear the ocean. I held that shell to my ear and heard whisperings of gypsies gathering up small children, rushing off with them. I see the tinkers playing those wild violin melodies that accompanied Bubbie in her Russian songs, the ones that surged through us both when the rush of the waves slowed down in the seashell.

I was almost four when Bubbie gave me that seashell when she stayed in Venice Beach during one hot Los Angeles summer when I came to visit her. I rode the carousel in Ocean Park, the horses spinning around, going up and down. Bubbie waited as I rode around each time.

"You remind me of myself as a child in Russia," she told me.

Like a slow gravity creeping up on her, she became frail, unpredictable, lapsing into a song or a sonnet in Russian. Leaning down in her yard to pick a dandelion.

"Don't ever forget, my *shana madela*," she said, "this, too, is a flower."

Bubbie would smile and hand me the flower, telling me, "Make a wish, my Jeanne, Queen of the Family," as we blew on the dandelion and the seeds scattered.

Bubbie and Zaydie lived in a white frame house on Avenue 52 and Baltimore Street in Highland Park, a suburb of Northeast Los Angeles. They moved there to that house in 1911, when they came from Sioux City, Iowa; before that, Omaha, where my father was the first child born in America. Before that, Russia.

The front porch had my special lawn swing that made cricket sounds as we rocked back and forth, the forest and rose on the faded cushions. Washed out and muted prints, like the grass when it has been without water, yellowed and unhealthy. Faded like Bubbie's lost dreams of playing in Russia, out free, coming in to have tea. Reading books in Russian.

Bubbie would put me to sleep with a Yiddish song: "*Ofyn pripechik vent a figural,*" or she would do index finger opposite thumb as her fingers climbed up and down.

"Do like this," as if a spider went up and down with her fingers index to thumb, index to thumb.

"Bubbie, what's it called?" I would ask her.

"Just try it."

I placed my pointing finger against the opposite thumb and then following it all the way up to the top of the sky and back down to the small gray kitten that came up to play with me when I called, "Kitty, kitty, meow, meow." I called her "HER" because that's what Bubbie said, HER, and then we'd both go up and down the spider web and then we'd both sing a grandma song about a place she called Russia, where her parents told her she was part of the aristocracy, a queen. She went dancing with a man she called Igor.

Igor, I liked the sound of that. EEE Gor.

"What's your name," I asked Bubbie, looking directly at her face. She'd taken off her glasses and it took her a long time to answer.

"Miriam," she responded.

"What kind of name is that?" and thought of *The Bible Storybook* to find my answer. Of course. The sister of Moses. The one who saved our people. That's Bubbie. It is so.

"What's Zaydie's name?"

"Samuel."

"Daddy's name?"

"Leo."

"Mommy's name?"

Bubbie stopped. I wanted to ask her again but the spider fell down into her lap as one hand held the other, then they both reached for me and Bubbie pulled me into her lap. She rocked me as we squeaked back and forth in the swing on the front porch as the kitten played with a string Zaydie gave me for her. We both cried but I didn't know why.

Bubbie continued to sing songs of her childhood. She said Russia was very far away and that sometimes late at night, when I was sleeping, she would go there and prepare afternoon tea. *Swee Touch Nee.* People gathered in her house with Zaydie and a man whom they said was a writer. Something like Doe Ski Ev Ski.

"Say this, 'Dostoyevsky.'"

I repeated the name, over and over.

I see Bubbie's hands with the itsy bitsy spider. Fingers chasing each other back to Russia, running free, free as I was with Bubbie on the lawn swing, on the front porch of her house, while Bubbie has gone far away back to Russia with Igor, Zaydie, and Dostoyevsky.

Conversation with Bubbie

I sit next to Bubbie. We push our feet on the wood floor on the porch, and back and forth on the swing, and she is next to me and I am happy. Then she tells a story with a special new word, followed by tears, then silence.

Funeral

I see the flowers on the front lawn. Roses, Bubbie calls them. "Smell," she says. Bubbie goes somewhere. I wish I could go with her. She comes back and sits next to me.

Smile

I know that Bubbie loves me. She does. I know. She knows. She is big. I am little. I sit here. Dad says she does love me and I am sure of it.

Dream

I am very little. I am in a basket being rocked back and forth. A face reaches down. Lips. Soft. A kiss. I smell that smell. Milk. Good. Warm.

Gone

Bubbie holds my hand. She has something to say. At first, nothing comes out. Then words. But no meaning. A song. I like a song. I follow it up and down. I dream we get up and dance.

Buried

Bubbie, what are these words? I don't know. I want some-body. She leans down and kisses me. She's right here next to me.

Gone

I feel her tug on my sleeve. But then there is no one. The breeze—warm. Summer. Nothing else. Sky, clouds. A sound. A bird singing. I want to be a bird. I know where they go. Where is Bubbie?

Floating

I am back again. My legs don't touch the floor. We slow down. "Bubbie, push again."

She comes back to me and pushes on the floor. We move. The kitten runs across the lawn. There is the wind again.

Never comes back

I know who that is. She knows me. She is here and not here. She sings to me but it comes out of Bubbie's mouth. Mommy.

Buried

The words don't come to me now. Just pictures. The car door, me. The windows. I can't see. Just the two of them in the front seat. Then just me—me next to Daddy.

Gone.

Bubbie, please, what is it? Tell me. Please.

Bubbie pushes again on the floor to make the swing go back and forth. She is sure it is what I want. But I also want the holes, the ones she goes through when she goes away.

"Daddy," I call out, as I see his car drive up. I don't know where I went or where Bubbie went. Right now we are all here.

1944

There She Is

I am sitting outside at the bottom of the steps in cousin David's backyard, right outside the back door. David is telling me a ghost story. I am almost four.

Why does David like to scare me? This time the ghost has my mother's name, Alice. And soon, while he's telling the story, I see her come flying down from heaven with a band of angels. She speaks to me, but David's voice keeps coming through. I should never have told him that I was waiting for a sign. Something that will tell me she is okay, that she is waiting for me.

There are noises from the cars up on Monte Vista. They're muffled and sound like the ocean tides. I keep waiting for my mother to ride in on one of these waves and come to me. David keeps talking.

"Tell her to say she loves me," I tell him.

"I love you," comes back in a voice that goes through him.

"And what else?"

"Don't be afraid." He hollers, "*Boo*" and jumps up laughing.

I steady myself and begin to cry.

"I'm sorry," he says as he puts his arm around me and we rock back and forth.

"Why did you scare me? She was almost here."

So we try again, David sitting very still and closing his eyes. "Tell her something about where you are," he asks my mother. Then the words come from his mouth and I hope it is my mother. She says, "In heaven."

"What's heaven like?" I demand.

"What's heaven like?" he repeats, and the words come out, "Ice cream cones and pancakes and angels and no naps."

I find this comforting. Much so that I tell him, "Ask her if I should come to heaven."

"No," he says. "You can't do that."

"Why?"

"Who will I play with then?"

"David, you have Jerry and Bernard and your mother and father. I have Bubbie and Dad."

"That's enough," he says. "How can you leave me? That's not fair."

"Then I'll talk to her myself," because my father told me she's in Chicago. But I say this just to make him mad.

"She won't listen to you," he says to me. "She needs me to say the words."

"David, do you love me?"

"Yes."

"Don't you want me to be happy?"

"I thought you were happy, here with me," he tells me and pleads, "Please stay here. Don't go to heaven. Please."

So I think for a minute, "Will you do anything I ask you to?"

"Yes."

"Can I have your teddy bear?" He hesitates, "Yes."

"Good, then I'll stay," and he goes into the house to get it.

For the rest of the day we just sit there on the stoop, and after dinner, come back and watch the stars come out.

"Look. See that real bright one?"

"Yes," he says.

"Good, there she is." We both nod in agreement, "Yes, there she is."

Roses

I was almost three when my mother left. Dad said she went to Chicago. She never came back. Bubbie's room became mine. I slept in a crib.

Someone walked into my room. She had a sweet smell of roses, like when I'd walk with Bubbie and we'd pick them. "Be careful of the thorns," she told me. We'd put them in a jar on the dining room table when we got home. I liked walks with Bubbie. There was no nursery school during August. I played outside all day. No naps. I never took them because people disappeared when I closed my eyes.

I ran out to Bubbie's backyard, crawling in dirt and high grasses, finding that furry kitten that smelled like garlic when I picked her up and held her to my face. I ran, jumping up and swinging from trees. Then it was time to eat rice pudding with steamed milk. My pants were full of dirt and grass stains. Bubbie told me they would never come out. Then it was time to go to bed.

Dad ran into the bedroom to wake me.

"Jeanne, Jeanne, this is Esther," he said. I blinked.

She was a magic angel as I opened my eyes. She was roses. She was soft like the kitten against my face as she leaned down. Dad told me they were going on a date.

"What's that?" I asked him. He smiled, the sides of his face rising up. He kissed me. He had a special perfume and soft skin, but not like hers or the cat's.

She smiled and told me, "Your dad says nice things about you."

The sides of my face went up to match my father's. I remember asking her to stay over and offering her my crib. I faded into evening.

Then came Saturday when Zaydie would let me go to his small store. Dad walked in to wake me.

"Dress in your blue pants and the tee shirt with the rainbows," he said to me. "Don't forget your socks and shoes."

Then Dad smiled. "Mozart," he said, "and Beethoven," and began to hum them to me. He told me they went to a concert under the stars at the Hollywood Bowl. They would take me there sometime.

I noticed a change. Dad said "we."

"When can she stay in my bed?"

He said, "Not yet."

"Do you like her?" I asked him, soft like the little gray kitten.

Saturday was the day I went to the movies after my visit with Zaydie at his store. Dad picked up David at his house and brought him over. I can still taste the popcorn and the orange, red, and green Jujubes that locked my teeth together.

David started to quiz me right after the movie ended and before Dad came to take us back to Bubbie's. "What about Roses?" he asked. I had told him that's what I call her and that my father and I would marry her.

Later that night, Dad drove up. He had on a white shirt and a tie, a suit for funerals and my cousin Bernard's wedding. He was telling me he'd met Roses' mother.

"Jeanne, Roses' name is Esther. Her mother's last name is Goldenberg."

I rolled it around, "Golden berg berg berg." It became a song that trailed the flight of the sun and settled into the warmth of dinner.

"I want her to live with us." I ordered my father, "Bring her." No answer. "Bring her to me."

My dad smiled. I saw his twinkle. Bubbie was glad.

There's a stop here. An insert. A missing mother. And a space in her stomach where the dead baby brother sat. There's nothing for this little girl. No explanation. Time is a lie moving away from the truth, away from the past. It is the distance from the excision, the scar cut from death to the current moment. The child screams in the early morning. She has no way to string anything together. A broken strand of fresh water pearls, the night blooming jasmine injecting its scent into her skin, her mother releasing and surrendering, mourning draping the window with a child's lullaby. In a simultaneous universe, mother and child walk hand in hand.

Roses sat out in the car. I ran to her. Dad went inside for his wallet.

"Open the door," I said to her, and I jumped in and onto her lap.

Time passed. They went to another concert, and then coffee.

"Jeanne doesn't know her mother is dead?" she asked him. If he didn't tell me, she wouldn't be part of our lives.

"There's a place in Hollywood," Dad explained. "Its name is Beth Olam Cemetery. There's a shelf up high and a piece of gold with black letters on it that say 'Alice.'"

That was my mother's name.

"I want to see her," I shouted. I didn't believe him.

There are certain words I could never say before that, words Bubbie said, like "funeral," "mausoleum," and "cemetery." If I were to say these words, bodies would float into the air. Hands would grab me by the neck and take me up to heaven, wherever that was, because that's what Bubbie told me when we swung on the lawn swing.

"Take me to her right now," I demanded of my father.

We got into my dad's old 1937 Chevy, the green color overcast with a coat of paint, more vivid than the memory of my mother.

I was quiet all the way there, not mentioning even one of those words because Dad might disappear again, because my grandparents might come and grab me away from him and hide me in the dark closet that smelled like my mother.

"This is a mausoleum," my father said softly as we drove up and went into a building with a stained glass ceiling the colors of all roses coming through, the lights refracting snapshots of my mother, my father, and me. The edges of the glass were faceted to sweep up all memories to the angels and send back soft rain, angels crying, mothers singing to their abandoned children, a father touching the hand of his wife as she left on that July 6 morning so early that not even the sun dared to show itself, ashamed of taking her away.

My father took my hand; we walked over to the long room, which held my mother, and her mother and father, in the wall behind a two-inch slab of marble marked with their names. My father lifted me.

I reached to touch the gold plaque as if I could grasp the scent of her skin or feel it soft and fresh in my hand.

"Mama," I cried.

Roses and the softness of kittens leaned down and told me her name was Esther. She was a dream in a cloud, the setting sky blue with orange, and the wind through the windows. Jasmine became Roses. A woman, a man, a child. They were taken up into one hand of God and gently tossed into the air. They were the sounds of yes and laughter. She filled my mother's absence. The mother who went on holiday. The one who never returned.

Queen Stinky

I

Before they go— my new mother and my father—
we take a ride in the car. They tell me they will be
back. "Soon." They say, "Don't worry, don't worry.
Aunt Elsie and Uncle Dave will take good care of you."

All smiles when we finally get there. Their apartment door is opened. I see my aunt and uncle. They are
smiling. Then the door closes. I continue to say, "See you
soon, see you soon," and run to the window and wave.
They wave back and get into the car. Then they are gone.

This place smells different. Not like Bubbie—
chocolate—or Zaydie—Ben Gay. Not like that. The
next thing I know it is morning.

"Jeanne." Aunt Elsie is by the door. It opens and
she comes in. "Time for breakfast."

"Why did they go?" I ask even before I eat.

"They went on their honeymoon."

"What's that?" I want to know.

"That's where people go when they get married."

"But we all got married. Daddy told me. He went
away and then they came back and he said, 'We got
married.'"

"Who?" Aunt Elsie says.

"Dad, Roses, and me," I answer rather irritated, because it seems like she just doesn't understand.

"That's right. Now, let's have some fun," she says.

"Time for breakfast." I'd better be good. I get up and go into the kitchen. I sit on a chair that has two pillows on it and I am almost high enough to reach my bowl.

Cereal, bananas, milk.

There is no one else here. Just us.

"Aunt Elsie, when will they be back?"

"Before you know it," is all she says and I begin to count on my fingers when the night comes and the morning comes.

"Breakfast." It is the third day.

"When...?"

"When what?"

"...will they be back?" and by the time I have counted all my fingers on one hand, I begin to worry. I do what I can to be good. Brush my teeth. Wash my face.

There are no other children here. I am alone.

The fourth day on the other hand, Uncle Dave says, "Let's go to the beach," and I know that means to see Bubbie.

My grandmother is there. Uncle Dave opens my door and I rush to her.

Home. It is almost like home, smothered in her arms. Bubbie always smells like chocolate. I want some. "No, you don't, honey," Bubbie says. "It's not real chocolate, just medicine."

We go on the merry-go-round, eat peanut butter and jelly sandwiches.

"I love you, Bubbie," but I still want to know, "When will they be back?"

"Soon," she tells me. Aunt Elsie adds, "Before you know it." And I know it is already past that, past what I want.

"I want to go home to Mommy and Daddy."

"Soon. Now, let's take a bath," Aunt Elsie says to me when we get back from the beach.

"No," I scream and run away from her and she chases me around their house with many doors. A dog barks. A mother calls someone but it's not my name.

I am at the big front door and I want to run out but I can't reach the handle so I can't get out.

"I want to go get them," I cry to Aunt Elsie when she finds me.

"No. Come back and take a bath."

"No. No."

I go to bed in my old clothes and I don't take a bath and again I don't take a bath and pretty soon I ask Aunt Elsie, "When will they come back?" Now I am stamping my feet. I throw myself onto the floor. She won't touch me.

By now I have only one more finger left to count on and I don't know what I will do next.

"No cereal. No milk. No bananas, not even straw-berries," I shout at breakfast. "I won't eat."

"It won't look good if she's starving and stinky when they come back," says Uncle Dave.

"What can we do?"

"I don't know, but if this is what having a child is like, I don't want one."

I hear the trail of the last words and I think, *Queen Stinky. I'll be Queen Stinky.*

I think about Queen Esther because I know that she saves her people but who saved Queen Esther from being killed? Then I remember it was her Uncle Mordechai. Uncle. "Uncle Dave," I say to him as I burst into their room. "Where are they? When will they be back?"

"Soon."

"No, it's already soon and then again soon," I tell him. I hear him get on the telephone. He talks for a long time and I can't hear him now.

I'm very scared. I itch because I won't take a bath. I am hungry but I won't eat. They'll be sorry, and I get into bed and pull the covers up over my head and in this dark place I am safe.

When I come out from under the covers, it's morning.

Aunt Elsie calls to me, "Jeanne. Breakfast."

I come out, "When? When?" I say.

"Tonight they'll be back," she assures me.

"No," I shout.

"Okay, then. Can I give you a bath and put on a fresh clean dress?"

"No," is all I say. I don't believe her.

II

It's happened. Mom and Dad are back. We are in our new place. A family. "A bath," Mom says. Just like that. No yelling, no words, just a hug.

"Follow me. This is your new bathroom. It's special. I decorated it just for you."

I go into the bathroom filled with beautiful tiles.

"What's that?"

"Purple."

"And that?"

"Creamy yellow."

"And black," I say.

"Yes, and black."

It is what I have been missing. I hear the sound of the water and see it filling the bathtub. My eyes dance around the room. *Mine*, I think, *mine*. For me. Special. I am about to take my first bath in a long time. Mom lifts me up and places me in the warm water, her hands soft against my skin. I sit. I think. She will be mad at me because I'm so dirty. But she isn't. She touches me with a soft wet rag, washes my neck then my arms and on my chest.

"Jeanne?"

"Yes," I answer. It feels good. She is here and I look up at her then all the colors. They are dancing around and singing to me. The song has no words. It's just like the angels. I am here with my mother and she touches me. Then she takes one foot and then the next foot. She dips the rag into the water. I chase bubbles with my fingers and take them and put them on my heart. "I love you," I say, and she begins to cry.

"Why?" I ask, "why?" and point to her eyes.

"Because I have wanted a little girl just like you for so long. I love you, too."

She laughs then I laugh and my hand pushes the water and she pours some over my head.

"Shampoo," she says, as she first rubs it between her hands and then into my hair.

"Will it make me cry?"

"No, it's Johnson's Baby Shampoo. Just for you."

Again those words. "Just for you."

"Yes," is all I say. I feel the warm water then her hands and I love her touching my head and then my ears. "It tickles," I tell her.

"Good," she says and then more water and more. The tub is full of bubbles now and I look at her. This is all I want. No more.

The colors make me happy. Purple, creamy yellow, black, dancing around the room.

I am here with my new mother. I am home.

1945

The Caves

I

I walk down to Sixth Street with Grandma Goldenberg, my new grandmother. She lives a block away from us on Cloverdale, she says.

When we get to Sixth Street, I ask her what all those steps are that disappear into the ground. "They are steps down to the caves," she tells me, not knowing how else to describe them.

"When the war started they were building places for people to live, and they stopped to go over to Germany to defend our people."

"The ones in the magazine?" I ask her.

"Yes," she tells me, "the ones in *LIFE Magazine.*"

As I walk down Miracle Mile with Grandma, she points out the shoemaker. The cleaners.

Grandma takes me to Orbach's Wednesday sale, where I see two or three mothers rip apart a blouse because they all want the same one. I think about the story of King Solomon with the baby. Grandma calls this store "The Snake Pit."

Grandma and I go to the La Brea Tar Pits. She tells me about when the giant sloth and saber-tooth tigers lived and where their bones were trapped, intact. She tells me they wandered there 40,000 years ago, a time so ancient and yet so real to me then that I could close my eyes and see them moving, the bones reconnected with the flesh, tigers slowly stalking prey, stopping to capture the sloth, then caught in a spell woven in another world and time.

The La Brea Tar Pits are a special place like my caves. I can sit there thinking while hiding away the dead, I can bring them back one grain at a time.

Before Yom Kippur, I think about the dead while my mother and my father make a list of those in our family to be remembered. Maybe I will find some of them down there in the caves, too.

The caves are a safe place. A place where I don't worry about being found, and so dark nothing could be seen, only light at the very top of the stairs, except when people walk by.

I am on a mission. I must find the dead. I must talk with them and see if they will come back. I don't know how I will do it. My mother says we can pray to the dead but that doesn't guarantee anything.

So Ronnie, who's six, and I go down to the caves, after we help our mothers with the dishes. Ronnie lives downstairs. My mom tells me to tell him that he has to hold my hand. She gives me her watch to give to him so we can be back at lunchtime. When I see him I tell him what my mother said and give him the watch. We walk outside and carefully look both ways as we cross the two lanes on Sixth Street. We turn left and cross over to the other side, go down the block, and then step into darkness, into the caves. We begin with a prayer. I tell Ronnie he has to cover his eyes to make it holy. Ronnie prays to his Uncle Sam and his Aunt Gertrude, hoping that they will talk to him.

"Dear Uncle Sam, I know you are in heaven and that Aunt Gertrude is there with you." He stops and looks at me, then continues, "How is it there? How are you? I hope God is good to you."

I pray for my first mother, who by now must be an angel because she's been gone such a long time. I also want to know about heaven.

After he finishes his prayer, Ronnie hears a sound, like the wind. No words, no notes, nothing. So then I say my prayer and for me, too, there is no answer. It has been this way for weeks now. Every day we start with a prayer and every day we get no answer. So I tell Ronnie, maybe the angels are on vacation, like I will be next week, and he tells me he will come down every day and say the prayers for both of us, because if we stop we will never get an answer.

Ronnie asks how I know the dead will talk to us. I tell him my mother says that the dead are buried in the ground, somewhere called Beth Olam Cemetery, in a place called Hollywood, the same place my father tells me I was born. He also tells me that Hollywood is the home of the stars. "Movie stars," Dad says, "like Clark Gable and Van Johnson."

"And like Orion?" I ask.

"No, those are real stars in Orion, not Hollywood stars, like Rhonda Fleming," whom he really likes a lot. "But still stars, I guess, like in the constellation Orion, the Warrior, made up of many stars," and Dad shows me Orion in a book called *Astronomy*.

"Have you ever seen Orion?" Ronnie asks me.

"No, it comes out when I am sleeping."

"So what will we do down in the caves today?"

"Listen."

"What for?"

"People that were here before us."

"Like dead people?" Ronnie says, because his Uncle Harvey died a while back and he knows that because he went to the park where they put his uncle in the ground.

"Was it scary?" I ask.

"No, not really. He just looked like he was sleeping."

"So maybe we'll hear him down here," and I make a sound of snoring and we both laugh and for the rest of that morning we sit very still on the dirt with some light coming down the stairs, and wait.

"Is it time yet?" he asks.

"No, not yet. First, we must talk to the dead."

So I tell him to ask his Uncle Harvey a question to see if he answers. All of a sudden we feel the ground shake and hear a dull sound of the earth moving and we grab onto each other and scream.

Then as quickly as we came down the steps, we run back up to the light.

"It was a big truck," Ronnie says, relieved, and as we see it drive down toward Fairfax, we both begin to laugh.

"How do you know for sure it wasn't Uncle Harvey?" And, sure enough, he thinks for a moment, and says he feels it just may have been a sign.

II

I step out onto the sidewalk, determined, and not a moment too soon. It is March 1945 and Ronnie is coming down the walkway. We rush over to the caves in Park La Brea Towers, two blocks away from our apartment building. It is during World War II, during my childhood bound by destruction and the killing of Jews. No one talks about it, but I know. I'm four years old and I know. I see pictures in the Los Angeles newspapers of naked skeletons walking. They have names attached to them, *Juden*, what the Nazis called the Jews: the walking dead. I form the picture of them in my heart and it's them I take with me to the caves. I can hold them close to me and protect, warm, and feed them like my new mother is doing for me. She is making meals. It's not like with my dad's mom, where I wouldn't eat because I had an ice cream cone in the afternoon and then at nine o'clock at night or so, I would ask for a bowl of Rice Krispies because I would be hungry. Now my mom makes three meals a day and they are good.

I take out the picture with the walking bones from *LIFE Magazine*. I bring crusts of toast and a bit of oatmeal I've wrapped up in my paper napkin, and I scrape it off and feed them like I do with my doll, Susie. Soon I will see them laughing and dancing and happy. Then it's time to run home for lunch.

Ronnie is always ahead of me and I let him go as I fold the picture and place it in the corner of the cave room under a rock I found in Bubbie's backyard last Saturday. I took the rock before she came out and saw me playing with Big Red, her cat who was in the weeds under the large tree my cousin David and I swing on.

It's here in the caves I place all of this and each week I bring another stone until I have a little pile. It's here I carefully remove them one at a time, unfold the picture, and smooth it out.

"They're going to declare peace," my father announces when he comes home from work at Lockheed where he helps make the B-37 bombers. Men who were not accepted into the army didn't have to go to war but had to do their part.

"They're actually going to declare peace and let all the soldiers come home," he says, excited.

I ask him, "What about all the people in the picture?" and he wants to know what picture. I can tell he's upset now. "Never mind."

The next day when I come home from the caves, which my mother reminds me are actually basements of apartments that they stopped building when the war broke out, I bring out the picture, unfold it, and place it on the table before dinner is set out.

"These people. What will happen to them? Where is their home? Will they come back with the boys?"

"So many questions," my mother says.

I shout out halfway through dinner, "You never did say what's a Nazi. Who are those children, the ones smiling at the man with the mustache? Can I wear a uniform like them?"

My father sits there, stunned, not knowing what to tell me, as I walk over to the *LIFE Magazine*, sit down, and continue to turn the pages.

Dad ignores what I asked. He says the war ended, but nothing has changed. He tells me how the Miracle Mile was started by Jews just like us. "Back in the 1920s," he says.

I want my miracles to come out. I've waited and waited. Nothing's happened. I continue to hope. I'm four years old and, after all, I'm on a mission.

Orpheum Theater with Grandma Goldenberg

The red trolley car stops on Broadway after picking us up on Wilshire Boulevard. There is a metallic twang to the bell. An abrupt stop lands Grandma and me at the street where the pavement is uneven. There is some motor oil from automobiles on the ground. I see the bottoms of my shoes reflected in it as I jump off the trolley and over it. We walk toward Spring Street and the Orpheum Theater to see the movie *State Fair.*

The lights come up on the marquee just as we round the corner. Maybe they see us coming. The excitement makes my heart pound, the blood racing back and forth from my feet to my fingers on my right hand, which Grandma holds in her left one, big and safe. As I pull her along toward the theater, we continue our talk from last week about the movies. I bring to it all my rhythms, tunes, and dreams from the movies I saw with my mother on what she called the big silver screen, and from the stories Grandma told me about vaudeville. She also hums melodies to me from the movie that we are to see.

"Grandma, what's that called?" I ask.

"'It Might As Well Be Spring,'" and she continues her humming.

The ticket counter is tall. I can't see up to the window. All I hear is the tear of hard ticket paper.

Grandma pays for the tickets, and I recognize the click of coins: a quarter, a nickel, and a few pennies. I know these from Bubbie's change purse and Zaydie's grocery stand, where I help him during the summer.

Air pushes against my body as I move toward the entrance. The tall man whose head touches the sky takes our tickets at the door.

Inside there are red, yellow, blue, gold, and green lights. The whole lobby, as Grandma calls it, is washed in light. Gold, but not like Grandma's ring she wears on her right hand, the ring finger. She always tells me that a vein from the finger goes straight into the heart. That finger presses against mine as we move through that place. But the gold of her ring seems so soft, as if I could put my fingernail against it and write the first three letters of my name.

"Jeanne," a voice breaks in. It's Grandma. "Do you want candy?"

"Jujubes," I tell her. I already imagine my teeth sticking together with red, yellow, and green. Grandma also gets us popcorn. I hear it being popped and smell a butter smell, like when Grandma fries me some eggs.

Music comes out from the large room behind the doors as we open them and push through curtains, which are soft on my hand as I run it up and down the cloth. It feels like the kitten my friend Ronnie has at his apartment.

Grandma says the large place way up at the front is the stage. There are a lot of people in the little floor below the stage, like my caves but without a top. It sounds like on the radio.

"That's the vaudeville orchestra, and that's the violin," Grandma says. "Pay attention," she tells me.

We walk slowly toward the front down the aisle. This is like the carpet in the story of the Arabian Nights, the one that flew. I push my feet down hard to see if the sky will come up through it.

I gather up colors from the candy and popcorn and put them in my pocket for Mommy when we get home. The lights go down and we wait for the vaudeville acts and the movie to come on. I'm safe here with Grandma and in this time I do not feel lonely or alone.

1946

The Remembrance of Trees

I learn to love trees from both of my grandmas. Especially Grandma Goldenberg, who teaches me to hug a tree and take it in as a friend, make it a member of the family.

Mom, Dad, and I moved away from Miracle Mile to Eagle Rock, from the big trees with the bark that peeled away, like papyrus, Grandma tells me, and into the yard with hibiscus and rose bushes and night-blooming jasmine and a large area with grass. There is one tree in the backyard whose leaves I play under many hot days in July, August, and September. Mom and I sit on our lawn swing, the one with the umbrella top, and she reads a book. I bring one out, too, so I can sit and read with her. It's the one she got for me on sale at the May Company in downtown Los Angeles. It was larger than the *Grimm's Fairytales*, but the words were still too hard. The one with the drawings of Humpty Dumpty and lots of nursery rhymes is the one I love because I can pick out words here and there.

When the blackbirds build their nests in the sycamore tree and have babies, I run out the back door from the kitchen to the lawn swing, quickly because the blackbirds think there is danger, and swoop down and peck my head if I am too slow, to keep me away from the nest. The birds don't know I am small and can't get to them. But there I am, sitting smugly on the swing, the times I beat them over to it. They call out to me, *caw caw*, and squeak for what seems like a long time, until we all settle down. I sit reading what I can and look very hard at the pictures for clues of more words, and the blackbird mom keeps feeding her babies, because when she stops, they squeak and tweet until she again begins to put food in their open mouths. I wish I were taller so I could see her feeding them.

The only chance I got to see a mother blackbird with her babies was in the nest she built in the awning by our breakfast room. But before I could see the mother feed her just-born bird babies, the neighbor's cat came over and climbed up and killed them right there in front of me. So I think, *Better I don't see these blackbirds.*

When the cat killed the birds, I wanted to bury what was left of them in the backyard along Lupe's and my fence, in the cemetery, to give them "a proper burial," but my dad said, "I'll take care of it," and picked up what was left of the nest and feathers and threw them into the incinerator. When my mother lit it, I heard the screeching sounds of dying birds billowing out with the smoke as it came out the top, cries of children and their mother, because the cat killed them all. I remembered something of a sound from long ago but couldn't put words to it. Each time Mom burned the trash, only sadness came up and, with it, tears.

October

I am six. This is the house where my mother died. The house is big. It sits on a corner. My mom tells me, "Be careful, there's danger where the streets meet."

The house has a graveyard where I bury all the dead things, along the fence line between Lupe's house and mine.

Someday I'll have a dog or cat and not just fish Mom flushes down the toilet because they get to God that way. I think there must be a ladder or an escalator like at May Company that takes them right up into the clouds, right into heaven. But the turtles, Theodore the Second and Theodore the Third, are different. The first Teddy Roosevelt, the twenty-sixth president, my father tells me, was a Rough Rider in a very early war. Theodore the Second and Third, my turtles, didn't get flushed away. I buried them in the flowerbed.

The graveyard is close enough to the fence and far enough away from the incinerator that I can still empty the trash and not step on the dead. I know it is impolite to step on them. The dead know who you are. They can see up through the dirt, can come and get small children and eat them up until there's nothing left. Not me or my hair or my eyeballs or the white rickrack on my red sun suit or the bag in my hand am I supposed to put into the incinerator.

Sometimes I just want to jump into it and see where all the trash goes. Like Dad's newspaper he rumpled and Mom straightened perfectly again.

"Always put the pages back in order so other people can read them," she tells him.

Mom asks me about the little piles of rocks that I put down one next to the other. "Markers," I tell her. Otherwise I might forget and step on the dead and they'll come and get me. Then Mom will worry and I don't want to make her worry because then she might get mad and leave. So I have to be very careful.

I spend all day trying not to step on the wrong place. I do as I'm told, brush my teeth, say, "Yes, ma'am," and "No, ma'am," fold up the paper just so, and eat all my vegetables. Never speak unless I am asked a question.

Except to Susie. She's my doll. I can tell her anything. She won't tell. I wish she had real hair, not just painted-on hair. It is cracking at the edges. Sometimes I look in the mirror to see if that is happening to me. After all, that could happen and then some of the secrets could leak out and then Mom would know how scared I am and how I can't sleep sometimes because I hear the turtles grumbling and waiting to eat me.

When it starts getting light and I can see, that's when it's safe to go to sleep.

My Friend Sammy

I press my finger into the notepaper to make a mark. Mom asks me why I do that. "To write a word," I tell her.

"Why not use a pencil?"

"Because then everyone would know and this is a secret place," I say, as I continue making indentations on the page, not wanting to reveal that I am actually writing a story and it's a surprise.

I make up stories and mostly tell them to Susie. She is a very good listener and since I swear her to secrecy, she never tells anyone.

This is the story about a little girl who is out in the middle of the forest. She doesn't have a mother or father, or a brother or sister, and there she is, so afraid. Then one day a dog comes and finds her, and takes her to his house.

The dog in the story is big and white, sort of like Sammy, the dog that lives behind the fence on York Boulevard. That's where Sally lives, on the way to the grocery store where I go to buy my yo-yo strings. Although Sally shares Sammy with her neighbor, he is really her dog. I go over there with my cousin Martin, who is staying with us now, and we eat figs off Sally's tree and give some to Sammy.

Sammy is my friend. In my mind, in my secret story, written in code on the paper with my fingernail,

I live with Sammy and his wife and children and I'm not lonely.

So one day I ask my mom if I can have a dog and my mom says, "No," because we don't have room.

"He can live in the backyard and we can build him a house."

My mom tells me again that night that we can't have a dog right now.

"Then when?"

"You'll have to ask your dad," she tells me.

Well, I know then that it is not going to be, and Martin and I will just have to go and play with Sammy every chance we get, especially on Sundays, in the mornings, before we go to get Bubbie and go for a ride. Sally and her parents go to church, so it's just Martin and Sammy and me. It is a good thing that they have a big backyard where we can throw Sammy's ball all the way to the back fence, so he can chase it and bring it back. He also knows how to sit and lie down, and barks when I say, "Speak."

Sundays are especially fun, and I know this is the closest I will get to having my own dog. I don't know how I know this, but I have a strong feeling about it. One day my dad says to me, "You know why your mom won't have a dog?"

"Why?"

"When she was a child," he tells me, "a dog bit her. So she is afraid."

"But Sammy would never do that," I assure him, and say that maybe it would be good if Mom goes over there with us to see him.

Dad tells Mom about this and the next Sunday, Mom walks down there with Martin and me. We go into the yard first while she stands outside the fence. "Sit," I tell Sammy, and he does. "Down," I tell him, and he does and then goes over to get his ball. I throw it, and Sammy brings it back, only this time, he brings it to my mom at the fence. She carefully takes it out of his mouth and throws it, but never once sets foot inside the fence.

After that, Mom never says much about getting a dog, but never says we won't get one someday.

As long as there is Sammy down the street, that's okay. Mom actually asks Dad to bring home a box of dog cookies from his grocery store, which he does, so we can take Sammy a treat—first, of course, getting Sally to get permission from her mom.

The next weekend, Martin and I get up extra early so we can do our chores and take the cookies to Sammy.

When we get there, he is nowhere to be found. Later that afternoon, we go back over, thinking he must have stayed in the house while Sally and her family went to church. When we see Sally, she is crying.

"What happened?" I ask her.

"Sammy went to heaven last night," she says, hardly able to say the words to us and then she runs back into the house.

When we get back home, Martin and I tell Mom and Dad.

"Can we light a candle like we do for Grandpa Goldenberg?"

"No. After all, Sammy was only a dog."

She never says any more about it, but I know this is one time my mother really doesn't understand.

1947

The Magic Violin

My violin is not really mine. It's on loan. The brown wood smells like the trees in Griffith Park, down by the small river with the ferns. It is really old and smooth, not like the trees near Grandma's, which don't have much of a smell at all.

I sleep with my violin. I place the horsehair bow across the pillow above my head so the bow can rest all night next to the violin. I dream about Nathan Milstein's *Magic Violin*. Nathan is a famous violinist. His story is about a small girl like me who is learning to play her violin. It's the record my mom gave me last year when I started playing the violin in the orchestra at Delevan Drive Elementary School.

My father tells me, "Next year you will be like Jasha Heifitz, the violin virtuoso. He's a distant cousin and quite famous." Bubbie's last name was Heifitz before she married Zaydie and became Simonoff.

Bubbie told me about Yasha, the most famous violinist in the whole world. She told me he was her first and favorite cousin in Russia. I want my violin to be my best friend, like I bet Yasha Heifitz's violin is to him. Mine is red-brown wood and has two holes that look like S's, like the first letter of my last name, and strings, four of them. I still don't know the names of the strings, but I will learn them soon enough.

Mom says I have a fine mind and that I can do it.

Right where I draw my bow across the strings, there's powder that is sticky. It is from rosin. Rosin is from trees and my mom told me that when it grows really old, it becomes amber. I want to wipe the powder off carefully, mind you, so that I won't hurt the violin. I think that it could scream out with sadness. That's a word my mom uses. Sadness. It means, well, not exactly mad. Not exactly like it has done something bad, and I'm certainly not going to punish it. I want it to love me because, to tell the truth, I love my violin and nothing will stop that. "I love you," I say to it. I hold it like I see Rhonda Fleming's boyfriend does with her, in a swoon. "That's called 'caress'," my mother tells me.

If I can keep the violin, not just have my mother rent it for me like we've been doing, then I know I will always have a friend.

When I first learn to draw the bow across the strings, it sounds like Lupe's cat next door when the cat in the yard next to her, Big Orange, comes over to court her. That's what my mother calls it. But I've been practicing real hard and my teacher says I will get better and better, and he will even start to let the violin play a song. I am just here to hold it. The violin is really the one who does all the work.

Will I sing out and play the sounds like the little girl in my Nathan Milstein record?

I hope my father takes me to a concert. Mom says he will sometime soon and I can see a whole family of violins. We are like that, a family who sings in the strings of something special, warm and soft.

I draw my bow across the strings and listen very carefully. Pretty soon I make the music and I am part violin.

Mom reads me a story. I carefully set the violin back in the case, the inside blue and soft velvet against the wood. I place the bow in the other part of the case. When I close the case, I hear the bow talking to the violin. "Don't worry, I will watch over you and keep you safe."

When my mother thinks I'm asleep, she takes the handle of the violin case, sets the case down, and opens it. She lifts out the violin, holds it to her body, says a blessing, and sets it back down after she kisses it goodnight, just like she does me.

Kinds of Water

It's Mother's Day down at Arroyo Seco Park in the riverbed of the Los Angeles River. There are plants growing but not much water. I hear a sound. Rain slides down the sides. If I am here long enough, it will fill the river, like my father told me it did when he was a boy. Miriam's mother put Baby Moses in the rushes and I pretend I am looking for Baby Moses. Why would a mother hide her baby in a basket and put him in a river? I think about the basket my friend Ronnie has for Easter when they gather Easter eggs in honor of Jesus, who died and came back. I wonder why my first mother never came back like Jesus did when he was buried in a cave covered by a rock, like Ronnie told me.

While I'm looking for Baby Moses, I hear my mother's voice calling me—far off. I see her at the top of the riverbank and I try to get up the side to come to her. The more I try, the harder it is. I take two steps up, and slide down two, again and again. I'm going to die. I just know I am. I ask God to take me quickly and send me up to the angels where my first mother is, and where Moses and his sister Miriam are. All I can think of is music. I hear angels singing. I see them coming down to get me, wings beating fast and hard.

"Leo, Leo," I hear my mother shout and my father stops and then comes running over. When he gets there, my mother tells him, "Get me three picnic tablecloths." He obediently runs back to the tables where Aunt Sophie and Gertie are setting out the lunch. He shouts to his sisters, "Give me the table-cloths!"

"Leo, you're crazy," they shout back.

"I don't care. Just do it." Soon he is back at the top of the embankment with my mother. She grabs the three cloths. She knots them together, one after the other.

By that time, cousins Mike, Martin, Joey, and David are up there pointing at me and laughing because I am crying and wishing the angels would come more quickly. When my mother tosses down the end of the cloth, she says, "Tie it around your waist." I quickly do as I am told. The next thing I know, they are tugging and pulling me up the embankment and into the safety of my mother's arms.

"Don't ever do that again," she screams, showering me with kisses.

"I won't. I promise."

The day continues with a barbeque then softball, which my dad plays with my uncles. All I can do is sit by the side and pray to God. I have been saved.

A year later, cousin David goes with me down to the river to catch pollywogs. He tells me that the Los Angeles River runs across Los Angeles from the San

Fernando Valley to downtown. The sound of the river is like music Bubbie plays on her piano. As I try to catch all the notes, I am caught in a time when there is no time, listening to the babbling of the water as it comes from a faraway place into this park, where each year for many years after, my family gathers first for Mother's Day and then for Father's Day. Here the family sets out wonderful food—hot dogs roasting on an open fire pit, and watermelon for dessert.

Birds quickly pick out a worm in the moist river-bed, as Cousin David and I watch quietly off to the side.

"Listen," I tell him.

"I don't hear anything."

"No. Really listen."

"To what?"

"The water, the sound of the water." When he finally hears it, he stops and we both stand there in utter amazement, as if this is only ours and we are the only ones in the whole wide world who hear this, notes going up and down, cascading like the river. We stay this way for some time and when we hear his mother, my Aunt Sophie, holler out, "David," we smile at each other and know that we have found something truly special.

We never speak of this again.

That night, I'm Esther Williams. I sink my head below the water in the bathtub and open my eyes.

Burning. Then clear. Then I see my body, my small heart down there between my legs. I touch it and it moves a little.

I think, Esther Williams, my arms moving like a butterfly and my legs like the frogs David and I catch when they are pollywogs in the Arroyo Seco. The ones I sell two for a penny to save money for yo-yo strings. David chases me so that I slip and fall into the arroyo, the water slimy, and then I feel like a frog, kicking my legs out to the side and my arms trying to help me up. David hides. No one is there to help me. I'm afraid like when he tells me ghost stories on the bottom step of his house when I stay overnight. It's where we go before it gets light because we both wake up and I call, "David," and he calls, "Jeanne," and we decide it's fine to get dressed and go outside to see what night bugs we can find that have stayed out longer than they expected.

And sitting right there on the bottom step, David says my dead mother will come back and haunt me because I have found another mother and she will be mad because she didn't really die. She just went away because I was always so bad.

The music of the water goes around in the tub like water over the rocks in the river, the rain coming down, cleaning me. And my mom really did die and the new one came and I shout this out to David, even though he isn't here now because I know and he doesn't. It's only at night he can scare me, and in the day like today, he can't make me mad or scared at all because the sun blesses me, and just to prove it, it gives me little spots called freckles. These are kisses from the sun and God, and they march all across my face and I love them a lot. So I'm Esther Williams and I swim around in the water, feeling it, remembering, and being happy. I think of the sound of the water in the park. David and me standing there. The water that carried Baby Moses through the bulrushes.

November

I wax my birthday bike and ride it furiously around the block. The cracks in the cement sidewalk bump me a little but I don't care. I go faster and faster. It's a powder-blue Schwinn with the racing stripes. They're white and no air catches on us.

I lean forward as I see them do in the movie I went to with Mom, the one with Van Johnson. It was a war movie, she said.

Now I'm Van Johnson and I'm on the motorcycle, headed for the hospital ahead of the ambulance and Jeanne Crain is waiting for me there and I can't disappoint her.

Then I come to York Boulevard and Avenue 47. I want to go across the street but Mom says a car will hit me. But it's an emergency. The cars don't understand and don't stop. I'm the doctor and Jeanne Crain is the nurse and this is wartime again and I'm in Guam and my Uncle Itzy is just back from there.

I wear his hat when he comes to visit and he's coming today so I ride faster than even the leaves blowing off the trees and it's November and very breezy. It's not cold but I have to wear a sweater. I have to get there very fast because a life is at stake. That's what Van says, before he jumps on the motorcycle. I want a scarf and a leather jacket like his, with the scarf that blows out in back of him. I look back at my braids to see if they look like that scarf, and just as I turn back around, I see that I'm in the street but don't see the car.

I hear the thud. The car has hit me. I slide down the street bloodying everywhere all over the road. I feel Jeanne Crain and my mom worrying, both sides of their faces going down as I walk home with my bike, the back fender dented and twisted, the spokes in the back wheel all messed up. What will I say? Because I broke a very important rule: Don't ride in the street, and that is one promise that should never have been broken.

Tears well up and my heart pounds. My mother calls my Uncle Itzy and asks him to come right over. I have been hurt. When he gets there, it takes both him and my mom to hold me down to give me a shot. This is after chasing me around the block before he catches me. I tell him the rescue story and why I had to hurry to get to Jeanne Crain. He tells me he never had to do any of this in the war when the soldiers were brought into the medic area. I should try to be brave. Then he gives me a shot of penicillin, "To make it all better," he says. I sit still while he dresses the bad scrapes on my arm and hand. I cry less for the sore arm and hand, and more because my mother said, "Don't do it," and I did it anyway.

A Little Knowledge

Mom takes me downtown on the #5 streetcar to May Company. It's the beginning of the new year.

She says to me with much glee, "Come on, let's go," and we get off, go inside and up the escalator to the third floor, where they have toys, like my cousin Michael's erector set, and especially what I have been hoping for, a new Schwinn bicycle.

Up there, too, is what Mom has her sights set on, books. It's after Chanukah and Christmas and there are tables and tables full of books, all on sale, some with pictures. There is one that says *From the Pages of LIFE Magazine/Twenty-Five Years.*

"Look, Mom, here's a picture of people with cloth stars." They all looked like they hadn't eaten a day in their lives. "And what are these?" I ask, as I flip through the book.

"The yellow stars were for the Jews, the *Juden*," she tells me.

"Jews like us?"

"Yes, Jews like us."

I was four when I first saw pictures like these in *LIFE Magazine.* I remember hearing things about the war when Mom and Dad talked with each other about it. But I don't remember seeing a picture of the triangles before. And here are people wearing triangles, but no stars. My mom says it is hard to explain, but these people were different. The Nazis punished them, too.

My mother tells me that she only let me look at this book because I had been a "busybody" and got into the magazines anyway. I smile, proud of my accomplishment.

Then Mom takes me over to the children's books and I look for Nancy Drew because she was smart and a detective and also a girl, just like me.

"Not exactly," my mom says. "After all, Nancy is older than you."

"But I'm getting there," I tell her. So she lets me pick out a book about Nancy Drew and she finds one for herself, *The Stories of Shalom Aleichem*.

"Quite a special choice," Mom says, since May Company was not noted for having books by Jewish authors. She remembered his stories from her mother, who read them to her in Yiddish when she was a child.

"Mom, what's Yiddish?"

"A language my parents spoke in Russia, and one that my mother still speaks."

"But Grandma speaks English now. And she's studying to become a citizen," I add proudly. "She says she'll be safer that way. But what does that mean?" I ask.

"I'm not quite sure," she says, "but if Grandma says it's true, it's true."

My mother tells me she loves me as she looks down at me. I clutch the Nancy Drew book to my chest. She says, "If you've got a book, you've always got a friend."

The New Girls

I

All I know is that one day there is an empty house across the street because Sally and her family had moved out, and the next day, there are two girls, one who looks my age, playing on the front porch and running around the tree in the front yard and laughing. I can't hear what they are saying. One of the little girls has hair like mine, brushed and pulled in back to make two pigtails. The other one has curly hair, like my cousin Michael's friend, Brubsy, curly and really red. My hair is more like waves, like the ocean. Hers is like the crinkly ribbon my mother put on my present for my birthday just last week. Next week, on Monday, I will go back to school. I wonder if the girls will be there, too.

I come back into the house to tell my mom about them.

"Where are they?" she asks. I pull her by her hand out to our backyard, where I can see the girls between the slats in the fence, and my mother waves at them when they look over.

All day I think about them and imagine that they are here playing with me. Susie, my doll, becomes one of them.

"Well, how are you?" I say to Susie. "What's your name? Mine's Jeanne. Shall we have tea?"

I run into the house and get my little china tea set I got for my birthday from my cousin Clare. She's old like my mother, so my mom says to call her "Aunt," which I do. Cousin Clare likes that.

Susie and I begin. I fill the small teapot. It has little pink roses around the saucers and inside the cups.

"Some tea?" I ask.

"Yes." I pour Susie's cup first, and then mine.

"Sugar?" I take some of the sand from my sandbox with the tiny spoon that came with the tea set, and pour in two spoons full like my mother does with her coffee because I know Susie has said yes.

We begin one of our afternoons together, talking about the birds, and my new dress for Rosh Hashanah, and Susie's hair. The hair talk is really about the girls across the street, not Susie, because Susie's hair is painted-on and brown, more like the color of my hair.

I keep wishing that Monday would come faster so I could see the girls at school.

"They may go to Catholic school," my mother says. "You never know."

"What's that?"

"It's like the Hebrew school I went to when I was a small girl. But it's for Catholics, not for Jews. You learn religion, as well as reading, writing, and arithmetic."

"Why don't I go to a school like that?"

"Because we are the only Jews in this entire neighborhood and there isn't any school just for us."

I have to face it. There is no one else like me. I sit there lonely. What else to do?

II

Although I go out of the house to have fun and pick a bouquet of flowers, all the stops along the way distract me. I see the neighbor girls across the street get into the car with their mother. One sits in front, one in back. The one in back is the one with the bright red hair. I want to holler out to her, "Stop. Take me with you." I don't know where they are going, or for how long, or whether they will stop or continue on until they run out of gas. I don't know if they will ever return home. I don't know if I would be comfortable in the car. If the seats are soft like my father's car seats or rough like my Uncle Irving's seat with rips where you can pull out the stuffing to really get to the bottom of things. I don't really care.

My mom talks on the phone to my Aunt Minnie and all day long they call each other back and forth. Do they get anywhere, I mean, really? I can tell you what they talk about: Mike didn't finish his vegetables last night; imagine that. Carrots. Or maybe he liked the corn kernels, the ones with pieces of red, the same color as the licorice, the kind my mother gets out of a jar at my father's store. Or the small red grapes Lupe has growing on her side of her fence.

My mom asks the postman if he knows the names of the two little girls across the street.

He says, "Babette is the older girl" he adds, who's probably your daughter's age, and Roberta, Babette's sister, is two years younger." Neither of them is able to come over to my house. Not yet. Because I keep waiting for a good time to invite them over for tea with me and my doll, Susie. Then we would be four points on my mother's card table. Me with Babette across from me and Roberta across from Susie. I hope they don't mind that Susie's hair is cracking. That she doesn't talk much. But I know what she is thinking, the same as she knows what I am thinking. As simple as that. And I have a good life: My mother and I never have to worry that she might leave and I have Susie and at night my father comes home and, after all, isn't that really just enough?

I wouldn't say that I'm exactly lonely. I have my new friends and I tell Susie about them. One story after another and, at night, I have my father and my mother.

We are a family. I only know that I am very happy about that because my mother tells me that, during the war, even after, many children had no one because their parents were taken away to camp, not like the summer camp at the temple, but one they never came back from.

So I wait outside all day for the car with the two girls and their mother to return. I still don't have enough courage, as my mother calls it, to go over there when I see them pull up. I just figure they will know that I have waited all day for them, and they'll say to me, "We need a new friend. Please come over and have tea." Then they'll add, "Bring anyone you want," and I'll go inside and get Susie, make sure I have her in a pretty dress, and, proudly, with Susie in my arms, march across the street and go up to their front door.

When I knock, they will answer, "Come in, please, you are on time for tea," and for the rest of that day, I will be full of friends. I am not alone. No one has died. It is the perfect end to a perfect day.

Snapdragons

Mom and I plant snapdragons in the garden in front of the turtles, Theodore the Second and Theodore the Third, careful not to move the stone markers. "Please be very careful," I say to her and tell her I have my reasons.

My mother begins by moving the small containers of seedlings into the flowerbed. First we put the pansies with their small faces in front, and behind them the snapdragons. I picture real dragons but I only saw one of them once in a picture book my friend Babette had about a boy trying to slay a dragon. She told me the boy was a saint but I couldn't remember his name. A week ago Babette peeked over the fence and invited me over to her house. Susie was happy I had a new friend.

I think back to the markers and realize Mom must have seen me bury the two turtles out there in that isolated spot next to the fence. She must have had some thoughts about why her six-year-old daughter could think to do such a thing. After all, the whole family had kept death pressed between the secret pages of their unspoken book of the dead.

"God knows, she doesn't need to know about that," I overheard Aunt Gertie tell my father about my mother's death. Aunt Sophie, his sister, agreed.

My grandmother, on her own journey into another country called Dementia, did not have to have her say but just continued to sing Russian songs and tell stories about funerals, just as she had done when I was two-and-a-half years old and without the vocabulary to know what that first death meant. Even when my father showed me the wall that held my mother's crypt, the truth seemed as far away from what I was seeing as her body was from me after she died.

Even so, I am afraid of the graves, so much so that I never got as close to the turtles as my mother Esther did when she dug the holes in which she placed the seedlings. I agree to pour water in the holes with my small watering can. My mother gets me a silver-colored one. She tells me it is stainless steel. It's like hers but much smaller. Mom got hers from her sister, my Aunt Minnie, for her birthday. Her birthday was two days after mine but we didn't have a party for her like we did for me.

I begin to water. "Like this, Mom?" I tip the can just slightly so that only the smallest amount of water comes out.

"Yes, that's good."

After she places another seedling in the ground, she asks, "Do you want to put the soil back around it?"

It is dangerous planting there. We are too close to disturbing the dead. So I say, "No," and add, "thank you." Just like she taught me to say when someone offers me something and I turn it down.

I am out with Babette from across the street, looking at the flowers. The pansies are beginning to open. It had been four weeks and school is just about out for summer vacation. Then I'll be able to help Mom even more in the garden. I want to check in with the turtles to see if they are beginning to be annoyed. I don't hear any rumbling noise like the complaints I imagine the turtles would send out—grumble, grumble. So I hope it is okay with them to have what my mother calls adornments. I know that when we go to the cemetery on Memorial Day, we put flowers on the graves of those who have gone before us, as my mother puts it. Our pansies and snapdragons are like that. Flowers to honor the dead.

My mother tells me it's a good way to think about it.

Then one day, on Thursday, the flowers on the stalks begin to open and my mother picks one of them and shows me what a snapdragon does. It isn't like I thought it would be. She tells me to hold the flower between my thumb and my pointing finger and squeeze it. Sure enough, a mouth opens up and my mother begins to talk in a high, squeaky voice while I do this.

"I am a dragon. Watch me snap." We both laugh so hard she has to run in and go to the bathroom.

When she comes back out, I grab a snapdragon and she takes hers. We begin to snap at each other. It is fun. My mom said it's good to be silly again.

"What about the pansies? What do they do?"

"Well, the word is from a French one, *penser*."

"What does that mean?"

"To think."

I think about the turtles and what they would say. A snapdragon and a thinker, both in that very special place.

After the flowers root, I imagine the turtles holding them down with their small claws, trying to do their part in building this new life, to replace what went out of their own bodies when they were put to rest.

"What's that mean, Mom," I ask her, "'put to rest'?"

"Where did you hear that?"

"In school, from one of the teachers."

"What did she say?"

"She said, 'That's enough,' to two of the girls who were arguing with each other—'put it to rest.'"

"Oh, that means to stop," Mom says.

"But what about the turtles? They were put to rest," and it is at that time I tell her that both Theodores, the Second and the Third, are right there near us.

"Will this wake them up?" I ask.

"No, they're dead, Jeanne."

"What is dead? I mean, really dead?" I ask.

"Like the turtles. They are really dead."

"Like my mother, really dead?"

"Yes," and she pulls me to her and holds me, "like your mother." Then she says her name to honor her, "Alice."

I Used to Feel Safe in Temple

I felt safe in temple until Yom Kippur, the year I was seven.

It is the High Holidays and Mike, Joanne, Joel, Richard, and I, and sometimes my cousin David, go outside every once in a while because we have so much energy we just can't contain ourselves during the prayers, which seem to have no meaning. The pages are like thin tissue paper, the kind you wrap clothes in or a piece of crystal.

Outside on the sloping front lawn are two grapefruit trees.

"Grab a grapefruit and throw it," I encourage Michael, just to have something to do. It's late September and it's hot. Morning begins to droop down. I feel the heaviness like tears that angels hold. I want to get out of the heat. I walk back into temple but my mother and father say to me, "Not now. Go outside. This is *Yisker.*"

I go out the side door but sneak back in, curious.

Yisker is where you fill out cards with dead people's names to honor them. I found the list at home that my mother wrote, and I memorized it.

This is that list:

Alice Welcher Simonoff, mother of Jeanne, wife of Leo, daughter of Sophia and Harry Welcher.

Avrum Goldenberg, father of Esther, Minnie, Julius, Erwin, and Max. Husband of Miriam Goldenberg.

And someday Miriam Goldenberg would be on that list. I think about her. I want to stop time and make the clock go backwards. Grab hold of the little and big hands and run them around the other way.

I remember Grandma Goldenberg and me at the Orpheum Theater in downtown Los Angeles. Vaudeville acts and a movie, *State Fair,* with Jeanne Crain and Dana Andrews. Grandma Goldenberg and me walking down Cochran Avenue on the way to sit in the park and read. Grandma Goldenberg protecting me, holding back Mother's anger over one thing or another with me, saying, "She's only a child."

I search for Grandma Goldenberg in all the crevices of my memory.

I come back out of the temple before the grownups see that I have been in there through the whole *Yisker* service. I have an ache in my body, in my heart. My forehead is sweating, my eyes red and sore from crying. I have been visiting with the dead. Joanne comes up to me and asks what is wrong. "Nothing," I tell her. But I know soon enough the rest of my grandparents will be on that list. As I say the names of those already gone, I know my life has changed forever. I am seeing death in a new way.

About Second Grade

Mrs. Van Noy looks at me like I am doing something wrong. She doesn't know I am an only child and I don't have anyone to play with at home except my mother. In class I talk with other children and even hug them if I get the desire. "Desire," that's a word my mother taught me, but so far it has only gotten me in trouble and I mean big trouble. Not just "Jeanne, don't talk in class," but "Jeanne, please stop talking," followed by the dreadful sound of tape being pulled off the roll, zzzzzzzzzzzzsnip, and before I realize it, Mrs. Van Noy is in back of me and slapping a piece right across my mouth, mid-sentence. No doubt about it, it's hard for me and I can't breathe very well out of my nose because I have allergies.

For a while I'm afraid I'll die and then I just want to. To disappear, to go up to Orion's belt and hang on for dear life, and hope against hope that he will cut off the tape with his big sword and I'll be up there looking down on Mrs. Van Noy as she starts to search for me because she's in trouble. She's lost me. I am gone and my parents come down to school and say, "What did you do to our daughter?" And my dad lets my second mother do all the talking because she's better at that than he is. He gets emotional and cries because I am missing and that is not a good thing. People say only girls cry and my father certainly isn't a girl. I always wonder about his tears, what is hurting him and how come when certain songs play like "My Yiddishe Mama," he says, "My mother sang this," and cries. He tells me that, years from now, I will understand. He says it is like a badge of honor, of connection, the son to the mother. "Something you just know," he tells me.

In the classroom I find myself drifting off to so many things I can't hang on to even one. *The shame*, I think, *the shame*. And before I know it, class is over. Mrs. Van Noy walks back toward me and pulls the tape off my mouth.

"I'm sorry I had to do that, Jeanne."

"Why did you?"

"It's a lesson for you and the others."

"Shame," I say to her, "shame."

The Bundle

The bundle is tied up in a red and white ging-
ham handkerchief that Bubbie gave me. In it are
ten felt feathers from the Woodcraft Rangerettes for
good deeds: three brown, three orange, two blue, and
two green. I arrange these on my bed and throw in
the three marbles I got in a trade for the polliwogs I
caught last Sunday at Arroyo Seco Park. That's where
David and I slid down the side of the riverbed, which
had slime on the rocks like snail trails.

"Smells like a swamp," Mom said when I brought
the polliwogs home from the picnic in a glass jar. "All
mossy," she added.

Down in the arroyo I like to pretend I am with
the Yang Na Indians I learned about in school. I draw
their huts and teepees at home in the evenings after
dinner. And on Wednesday afternoons when the Temple Sisterhood has their meeting at Sycamore Grove
Park, my cousins Mike and Joey and I run across the
street and up the block to the Southwest Indian Museum, where we see models of the village of Yang Na
Indians who lived on that very land. I want to take my
best friend, Babette, with us but only Temple mothers
and their children can come to the meeting.

Babette isn't Jewish. I explain holidays to her, like
Chanukah, when we play *dreidel*. "Like a top," I tell
her. "Each side has a Hebrew letter and depending on

which side it falls down on, you get everything, half, or nothing at all and lose your turn." I also show her the three walnuts and two almonds I won last Chanukah plus the prayer for the lighting of the Chanukah candles cut out from the box my mom got from Israel last December.

This Chanukah, Babette gave me her small heart ring. That was so wonderful. I gave her my Captain Midnight Signaler. Now I can't play under the bed in the dark with my cousin Martin and signal him when we tell our stories to each other at night. Even so, I gave Babette that special ring because I loved her more than anything.

I want Babette to be a Woodcraft Rangerette and wear a band that displays coups and merit badges and come with me into the woods and sleep on pine needles and stored-up dreams.

I didn't get to go on that trip with Babette. I saw this one tree when the Woodcraft Rangerettes went up to the mountains on a weekend trip to search for berries and learn their names. The berries were sweet and sticky in my mouth; I can still taste them sometimes.

"Babette," I ask, "what's the difference between a Girl Scout and a Woodcraft Rangerette?"

"I don't know," Babette says.

I rush home to ask my mom and she tells me I ask too many questions. She tells me it's something a child wouldn't understand. Then says, "You will carry this knowledge with you like a bundle in your heart."

I go back to the same question. "Mom, what about the Brownies? What about the Girl Scouts?"

My mother says she has to make another phone call. That it isn't too clear. That the answer she got from Mrs. McKinzie, my third-grade teacher and one of the Girl Scout leaders, and Mrs. Van Noy, who had been my second-grade teacher, distressed her.

I begin thinking maybe my mother didn't leave. Or die. Maybe the Nazis in the pictures in the magazine took her and she couldn't get back because she was in a prison cell, and not being burned like the witch in Hansel and Gretel my Uncle Max read to Martin and me. Mother's family in the camps probably never heard the story of how Gretel tricked the witch and pushed her into the oven and, *poof*, she was gone, so they didn't know how to save themselves.

And my father, he knows the whole story of the war and why he was denied a teaching job, and no child would hear him tell it because he couldn't be a teacher, but what about me? Why can't I live near my friend Stuart from the temple, whose family moved to be with a lot of Jews in the Fairfax neighborhood? They don't have to worry about being tortured. All I know is that Mom says I just can't be told one more bad thing.

Mom tells me the Woodcraft Rangerette Indian way is better. "Los Angeles was like this a long time ago," she says. "The Yang Na Indians followed their own traditions before the missionaries started the missions." She says that the Indians found seashells in the ancient ocean bed below the first and second layer of soil and that they grew maize on the side of the river that used to flow near where the Southwest Museum is now. This connection the Rangerettes have with the people and the land is more ancient than any the Girl Scouts have to offer.

"You will learn knowledge that will be useful to you in your life," my mother says. She takes a piece of carob bean and three acorns, a packet of carrot seeds, and her father's watch fob, which she places in the red and white handkerchief. "These make powerful medicine," she says. "My father was a scribe and a rabbi, a teacher. He sat *Shiva* and mourned for the parts of the family destroyed at Dachau." She says I will understand when I grow up.

I feel my heart bending down and I try to pick up the throb from the earth. I tell Babette that something has died and I don't know what. I tell her my mother knows an answer that I'm ready for. I have a feeling that Babette's mother knows some of the answers, too, from her old home in Paris, that her family and mine are somehow connected. I don't have actual proof like a picture of the two of them when they were kids, because Babette's mom is from Paris and my mom is from St. Paul in Minnesota. But maybe her mom saw the same things mine did in *LIFE Magazine* in the pictures of Paris and the Nazis and the Jews and wouldn't that be something—maybe Babette's family even helped hide Jews in their basements so, in a way, we are almost in the same family after all.

I don't want to wait even one more second before Babette and I become blood sisters. It's at this time she cuts off a lock of her hair and hands it to me.

"For your bundle," she says. We sing a song and hold each other and rock. Pretty soon we are sleeping in each other's arms. I remember dreaming I saddle up a horse, the one on the carousel I ride with Bubbie at Venice Beach, and Babette and I ride free to the top of the hill by the Southwest Museum. We pick wild flowers by the old deep river bed; we stop and rake our fingers through the soil and turn up two seashells.

"Here," I say, "you take one and I'll put one in my bundle."

Babette is my loving friend. She is now my sister and we can celebrate the Jewish holidays with delight.

But the next day I wake up and I have a strong sense of why I can't be a Girl Scout. It's because I am Jewish.

I can hardly wait to talk to my mother. Tears redden my eyes and soak my hair and my neck. She finally comes into the kitchen to make coffee and sees me standing there and embraces me while I sob.

I shout, "I never killed Christ like Donavan says. I never hurt anyone."

My mother holds me so tight not even air comes between us. And she knows I understand. This is prejudice.

When he comes home, my father talks to me. "Jeanne, in Eagle Rock, where we live, in the country we now call home, certain things are not open to us. The Girl Scouts is one of them. And for me, being a teacher was another."

"Dad, didn't Bubbie and Zaydie come here because they couldn't be Jews in Russia?"

"They couldn't practice being Jews and be free."

"What does that mean?"

"They had to hide who they were."

"Why can't Jews be teachers?"

He holds me and says, "For no good reason."

One God

"Mom, Mom, there's going to be a program at school," I say as I come running into the house on Wednesday afternoon.

"What program?" she asks me.

"It's about Christmas songs. Babette knows all the words. She's Catholic and she loves Jesus Christ the Lord."

It was as if I had slapped her across the room. I see my mother's face as she tries to level it.

"Jeanne, sit down."

"But I want to go to Babette's."

"Just sit down," she says again, this time more insistent. So I do as I'm told. I remember the commandment: Honor your father and mother.

"Mom, both Babette and her sister, Roberta, are going to be in our school choir and go caroling. That's when you…"

"I know what it is," she says with tightness in her voice. I can tell she's getting mad. I try to think what I could have possibly done wrong because, to tell the truth (that's what my mom says to me all the time), all I want to do is be one of the girls who go caroling.

"Jeanne!"

I snap back into place like an erector set that one instant is a little girl sitting and in no time falls flat. I say, "Yes, Mom, what's wrong?" I make myself taller then cross my arms over my chest like I see Humphrey Bogart do in *Key Largo* when he's talking to Lauren Bacall.

"Jeanne?"

"Yes, Mom."

"What we have here is a religious difference."

"What does that mean?"

"Number one, Babette and Roberta are Catholic. Right?"

"Yes, that's right, but…"

"Stop. Listen."

"Yes, ma'am," I say and sit down, the wind of excitement blown right out of me because I know what comes next.

"You're not like other little girls."

"Yes, I am. Babette and I are both seven years old." Then I add, "Okay, so I'm a Woodcraft Rangerette and she's a Girl Scout."

"See, well, there's a difference already," she says. "And where do you go on Sundays?"

"To Sunday school," I answer. "And services on Friday night."

"And where does Babette go?"

"On Sunday, to church for services. So what's so different?" I ask. I can see that she is getting madder and madder at me.

"And, okay," she says as she straightens her skirt. After a moment of silence that fills my whole universe, she asks, "How many Gods are there?"

"That's a silly question. One, of course."

"How many Gods does Babette have?"

"I don't know."

 Then I consider what Mom tells me: "There's God and there's Mary and Jesus. Count them."

"Three."

"And do we believe that Jesus is a god?"

"No, but..."

"And what is one of the really big things God asks of us?"

"Thou shalt have no other gods before me," I say, still feeling really left out. I sit back down because I know the answer about caroling.

The Chanukah Party

I

"We're going to have a party for Chanukah," my mother says when I come in Thursday afternoon. Then asks, "Who do you want to invite?" and I think right away of Phyllis Brunson and Sally, who lives on York in the middle of the block with the wall that holds in her front lawn. And my cousins Mike and Joey.

"What about David?" I ask.

"If his mother will let him come. He has to get a ride." My mother doesn't drive, and neither does Aunt Sophie.

I know that Uncle Gordon will drop off Joey and Mike on his way to work since Christmas vacation comes right before the party and school will be out. That's good. No one will have to miss any school, my mother tells me.

I ask my classmates, one by one. I am getting really excited.

"Mom, I forgot to invite Babette and Roberta."

"Go and ask them right away," she says.

When I go running across the street, Mrs. Boyer is out planting flowers in her front yard, a camellia bush, she tells me. Then I know my friends, Babette and Roberta, will stay there forever.

"Yes, they can come," she says.

So the day gets here and I help Mom prepare potato latkes, a special pancake out of grated potatoes, that we have for Chanukah. I get out the special cut crystal dishes for the applesauce Aunt Minnie made this summer.

Mom and I sing a few Chanukah songs and light the Chanukah candles. One of the songs we sing, *Maotzur*, tells about the Macabees who fought the king for the freedom to take back their synagogue and practice being Jewish because the king said it was against the law. When Ginny and the others ask about singing Christmas songs, my mom says, "We don't do that." She explains that Jewish children don't believe in Christmas. I don't even know the words to the songs because, to tell the truth, I don't understand what they're all about, or Christmas with the birth of Jesus and the three wise men, and why would any mother and father live in a barn. Like my mom says, "Charity begins at home." Didn't they have an aunt or uncle or a neighbor who said, "Take my spare bedroom or even my living room. No need for your baby to have a straw bed and for you to be with the farm animals, the sheep and pigs, horses and cows"?

The party went beautifully and we ate all the candy, nuts, and latkes, as well as the cookies baked in the shape of the Jewish star.

We distributed presents to all of my guests. Mom and I were pleased. Mike and Joey went home with Uncle Gordon. I showed everyone what a Jew does that is special. I felt so proud, especially lighting the first of the eight Chanukah candles and saying a blessing over it.

"It's a good thing to be Jewish," my mother says, and I have to agree.

Each evening we light one more candle and on the eighth day, I get my special present.

"Open it," my mom and dad say.

I tear off the paper quickly.

"Don't you want to read the card?"

It's a dictionary. This is what I have dreamt about. The card doesn't matter, but I read it because they ask me to. It says, "To our daughter, may your life be filled with words of joy." And it's signed, "Love, Mother and Dad."

My life has changed forever. My friends stop coming over except for Babette. Roberta is two years younger so she doesn't play with us, anyway.

My mother gets thank-you cards from a few of the parents and the kids smile at school when we go back, but something has changed.

I try to think of what I could have done wrong and want to ask each and every one of them.

Phyllis Brunson, who lives a block away from us, stops playing with me after that party. She says her mother doesn't want her to be associated with me anymore. She is the only one who says anything and then just walks away.

When I get home and tell my mother what Phyllis said, she tells me she will call her mother or maybe just go over there, and does.

When Dad comes home at six o'clock, he washes up and we have dinner. It is brisket of beef, something that Mom usually saves for *Shabbas*, with the potatoes Dad and I especially like. Crispy on the outside and soft in the middle so you can sink into them and rest there like on my mother's soft feather pillow.

Dad tells us about his day at the store and adds, "I've hired a new man for the meat department, a licensed butcher," which means he can make the store bigger.

"Good," my mother says, but doesn't say much more.

After I clear all the dishes, we have hot baked apples for dessert with the juices flowing over the edges and a touch of brown where the cinnamon had been sprinkled and baked into the tops, so sticky and sweet that after Mom and I do the dishes, I keep tasting that sweetness.

Then I spend a long time opening my dictionary to different pages, looking at words, forming each shape in my mouth and then sounding it out loud.

Mom reads her book, one of the "Book of the Month Club" specials, a new one, she tells me, a mystery.

Dad reads the sports page, telling Mom the latest scores of different games, but she truly seems not interested in them, or in laughing at the funnies, and she frowns as he talks about the new gizmo Dick Tracy has on his wrist. When the clock gets to eight, Mom says, "Time to get on your pajamas and get ready for bed."

"Yes, ma'am," I reply, and take my dictionary into my room, where I place it right next to my pillow on the bed. Mom comes in and reads me a story, something about a girl with long, long hair in a tower.

Then all I hear when she shuts the door are words between the two of them. My mom starts crying, and I know I've done something wrong.

"I thought when my parents came over to this country from Russia, we would be safe," I hear my mother say.

II

After the party, nothing seemed the same. Not the way my mother combed my hair, not the way my father came home from work. Something had changed, but I didn't know what.

I went to school. I played and came home. Many things hadn't changed. Not the way Mom greeted me when I came home and we talked about school that day. Not the cookies with a glass of milk on the kitchen table, or the tablecloth that had flowers like Bubbie and I used to pick.

The air was crisp. I could almost touch it. I could taste a difference but I couldn't find the word for it, not even in the dictionary.

Charity Begins at Home

It's hard for me to think about Christmas at all since the Chanukah party. Joseph and Mary don't have any friends and Baby Jesus is born in a manger. Already I'm upset because it says in the Torah that pigs aren't kosher and there they are in the barn. Mary and Joseph are Jewish in a barn with un-kosher pigs, and our rabbi says be kind and welcome poor and hungry people into your home, feed them, and give them a place to stay. Mom insists that Mrs. Levine and her daughter, Rivka, who is as old as my mother, come over for Friday night dinner. Dad picks them up on his way home from his grocery store and then they stay and help my mother and father and me usher in the *Shabbas* Queen by *benching lecht*, lighting the Sabbath candles, and we wave her into ourselves and our home three times with both our hands. We either put a napkin on our heads so our heads aren't naked before God or sometimes my mom uses one of my dad's extra *yarmulkes*, especially the white one with the gold letters that we got at my cousin Bernard's bar mitzvah.

We have the blessing over the wine, which my dad sings, the blessing over the *Shabbas* bread, which we all sing, and then we eat brisket of beef with potatoes that have been roasted with carrots. For dessert we eat fresh fruit or peanut butter cookies with the X's from forks on the top. I can't have milk right then, at

dinner, at that meal, like I need to build strong bones
and teeth, like Uncle Whoa Bill on the radio tells me,
because Jewish people can't mix meat and milk. It's
in the same Torah portion that says we can't eat pigs.

Mrs. Levine and her daughter always thank Mom
and hug her before they go home with Dad and sometimes I go with them for the ride. The next time I go
with him to drop them off, I ask my father, "Would
you invite Joseph and Mary and their little baby Jesus
for *Shabbas* dinner like we invite Mrs. Levine?" and my
dad says, "Where did you ever hear about Jesus?"

"From the kids at school." He pulls me close to him
as he says, "Yes, I would. A *mitzvah* is a *mitzvah*."

"What's a *mitzvah*, Dad?"

"An obligation." He reminds me of the prayer on
Saturday mornings at services that tells about the
special commandments, like honor your father and
mother, and the rule to welcome the stranger. "A
mitzvah," he says, "is a blessing and a good deed."

Donavan

Donavan lives around the corner. He's in the same grade as me at school. I don't know why he has chosen to pick on me. It just isn't fair.

I want to kill Donavan. I hate him. He's ugly. And mean. I don't understand why he says this to me, "You killed Christ." I didn't. Every day on the way home from school and during recess, he follows me and shouts this at me.

I now have no friends who will walk home with me, except Babette. It is five blocks home and I don't want it to be like this. My mother and father tell me, "Don't hate anyone." Don't want to kill anyone because then we become just like Donovan. Just turn the other cheek, like it says in Babette's Bible, and I'm not even sure it says that in my bible, the Torah, because why would God want a child like me to be tortured that way.

I'm glad I have Friday night services to usher in the *Shabbas* Queen and begin our rest. She can walk with me when I think of her. On Saturdays and Sundays, Donavan doesn't call me a Christ killer because he is at home. Mom says that Sundays are for the Protestants and the Catholics, and my friend Babette is Catholic. Sometimes she goes to church when her dad is not too sick because he went out with his friends the night before, and came home mad. The next day

her mom doesn't look so good. Sometimes, though, I
see Babette and her mom leaving for church in their
Ford sedan and her dad isn't with them. Her mom
wears sunglasses like a movie star and I can't see her
eyes.

I wonder how many more days and weeks I will
have to listen to Donavan. I ask Babette if she sees
him at church and she says just once in a while and
when he says something to his dad, his dad slaps him
hard and it looks like Donavan is going to cry.

So when she tells me this, I think, maybe I don't
want to kill him. I am afraid of him, of his words.
What if it were really true after all? But I know from
my mother that Jesus was not a god but a rabbi and
a teacher, like my mom's father. He wanted people to
love each other and to be kind. Not to hate each other
and make each other scared. If Jesus were here today
I could go and talk with him and see if he could reassure Donavan that I didn't kill him. I am just a child
like Donavan. Then I begin thinking. I wonder who
told Donavan that terrible thing after all. Maybe the
same man that hits him.

What His Father Taught Him

It was like listening to the radio. My parents learned from one of our neighbors what Donavan and his father said about us.

"Those Jews are the ones with all the money. They are destroying our country, like the moneychangers. The ones who helped kill Christ," Donavan's father said.

"And you told me Christ died for our sins, didn't you, Dad?" Donavan said.

"Yes, I did."

"Who killed him, or did he kill himself?" Donavan asked, remembering the story his father told him about his friend Hank, who killed himself after World War II. But then the United States "had to save them. Damn Jews. Maybe Hitler had the right idea."

"What idea, Dad?"

"Killing all the Jews. After all, they were the ones who really killed Jesus. Those money-hungry Jews. Even back then, they were the ones who always tried to make better deals for themselves."

"Like Mr. Cohen at the store where you buy your work clothes?" His father said that Mr. Cohen couldn't be "Jewed down." "He always sticks to his original price," Donavan's father said. "Wonder who taught him that? Certainly not Jesus."

"Dad, what about the family who lives on York Boulevard?"

"Those Jews? The Simonoffs."

"Yes, them."

"Have you ever seen the father? The one with the big nose?"

"Yes," said Donavan.

"And his wife?" his father added.

"Yes, Dad, only when she hangs up the wash."

"I remember the first one, the fat one, the one who always sat outside just reading books."

"What's wrong with that, Dad?"

"It's obvious why she was fat. Didn't work a day in her life. Not like your mother, who worked at Lockheed during the war."

"When you were away in the army?"

"Yes, when I was out saving the country. What for? The Jews? Yes, that war."

"And what did that mother do?" Donavon asked.

"She died. I remember seeing the ambulance come take her away."

"And that's when the Jews moved out of their house?"

"Yes, and that was good because they were the only ones in the whole neighborhood," Donavan's dad said. "I was glad. Good riddance. And now they're back, goodness knows why."

"I go to school with the little girl."

"I know," he said. "Don't ever talk to her."

"Okay, Dad. But did she kill Christ?"

"Yes," he said. "That's exactly what she and her kind did and they won't be saved. They'll never go to heaven. They'll all go to hell."

"Will I go to heaven?"

"Yes, son."

"What can I do about bad people like them?"

"Remind them of their great sin. Remind them. Say it to them with every waking breath. Set it all right."

The next week after Easter vacation, when the whole family saw the Passion play at church, Donavan started it.

"You dirty Jew girl," he hollered on the way to school. "You killed Jesus. You Christ killer."

1948

What about Bubbie?

I

My mother and father had a conversation. I didn't hear all of it but I heard enough to know that something was changing again.

My mother said to my father, "So how are you going to tell her when it happens? And you know it will happen. She will probably die sooner than later. Your mother isn't getting any younger. She wanders off like a child, lost in an empty field in her own country, only she doesn't recognize it. Is that being well? In the middle of a sentence, your mother just stops. Now, is that normal?"

"No," my father said, unwilling to face the fact that it could happen anytime, that his mother could wander off one day and never return.

"It's just old age," he said as he struggled with the truth. "It's just old age," he said. "She's fine."

"Fine today," she countered. "What about tomorrow, or next week, or next year? Leo, face it. It could happen."

"The doctor said she could last a long time yet," he continued, his eyes tearing.

"Get a hold of yourself. You're a grown man."

"Yes, I guess so."

"Well, the man I married is."

He stepped back then said, "I'll be right back. Bathroom."

"So, Leo," she said to him when he came back into the room. "What's it going to take?"

"Give me time to think about it. If God is good to us, it will be a while yet."

"I'm sorry but God has nothing to do with it. I faced my biggest decision when you asked me to marry you."

"What do you mean? Didn't you love me?"

"Yes, but…"

"But what?"

She could tell she said something that hurt him.

"Leo, after all, it is your mother."

"I know, I know, and I should be strong, but…" he said.

"No buts. When the time comes, you have to be the one to tell her."

"All right. All right." And for the rest of the evening he said nothing else.

II

It Is the Time

Through the window I hear my mother and father arguing.

Right after that the phone rings. My father answers and I hear him start to cry and say, "Yes, Gertie, I'll tell her." And then he says to Aunt Gertie, "Do you need some help?"

He gets off the phone and turns to Mom, "No, I won't do it. I just can't," my father says. I think it must have something to do with me, because, after all, didn't they just tell me I was the most important thing in the world to them? Then they send me outside.

Dad comes out to get me where I am outside play-ing with Susie.

"Come inside now," he says. "I have something to tell you."

"What? What is it?"

He takes my hand and leads me into the house where my mother is sitting on the couch. She looks like a ghost, all white. My father deposits me in the chair facing both of them as they sit on the couch, stiff as the lines of the old Duncan Phyfe sofa on which they sit. My father's face is stained with tears. My mother takes her white linen handkerchief with the flowers on the edge and dabs my father's eyes. "Now, Leo, I know this is hard, but you have to tell her."

"First some milk and cookies," he says, trying to avoid this thing that is so difficult.

My mother moves both of us into the dining room, where I can see the hibiscus flowers. Their red petals bounce in the slight spring breeze outside the window. I love that color. A hummingbird is drinking from the flower as I start to sip my milk, followed by a bite of what is to become several cookies, as my father set-tles down, crying without stopping, in his chair next to me and across from my mother.

"Just eat the cookies," he says with tears in his eyes. The crying has stopped as he tries to drink his tea. He can't eat the cookies. I have never seen him unable to eat.

"Well, what is it?" I ask, looking over at him. I figure that Mom has given him the job of telling me whatever it is. I can only imagine what he is going to tell me, what is making him cry.

"Bubbie is dead," he blurts out.

I holler, "Bubbie."

My mother comes over and draws her chair right next to me and holds me to her. "Your dad has a hard time saying the words, you know."

I don't know what will come next and am glad when my father gathers us both to him then grabs the tin of cookies, the one with the yellow roses on top that Bubbie gave us, and we all go out to the car.

"Where are we going?" I ask. Father pulls out of the driveway.

"To Aunt Gertie's. Everyone's over there now."

When we arrive, I get out of the car quickly and run into the house. I jump onto Zaydie's lap. Zaydie sits there, his blue eyes blurred, his white hair uncombed, his beard the stubble of day-old growth.

"Oh, Zaydie," I say to him with tears in my eyes, "what will we do now?"

Jews Don't Have Saints

Jews don't have saints. But Babette keeps telling me about Saint Anthony and Saint Joseph. Saint
Pasqual hangs on her mother's kitchen wall above the
Gaffers and Sattler 1940 automatic oven and griddle,
above the pot of simmering soup, above us as we sneak
around getting our share of the chocolate chip cookies
hot out of the oven.

My mom is not big on chocolate chips, but makes
peanut butter cookies with the cross fork marks on
top, first one way, then the other, like a checkerboard
out almost to the edges, where the cookie is slightly
fatter and softer. She makes mandelbrot, a large log
of dough sweetened but not too sweet, with walnuts
mixed in. Once it is baked, Mom slices it in strips,
puts it back into the oven to crisp, and then sprinkles
it with cinnamon.

I want to know about the saints: Saint Mary and
Saint Bernadette. I want Babette to tell me about
them. I tell her none of them are in my bible. She says,
"Yes, they are," and she brings her bible over to show
me.

Not only am I missing a whole book that includes
Baby Jesus and Christmas, but a lot of people who
were with Jesus, she says.

And I say, "Who is Jesus? My mother told me he's
one of your three gods."

"It's hard for you to understand," Babette says. "He is the son of God and real important," so much so that Babette's parents hung him on their wall next to Saint Pasqual, nails in his hands to hold him, blood gushing out right in the middle of his palms. Babette calls it "the lifeline." That's what her mom told her. There are nails in his feet, too, right on the part where mine get all brown from my sandals where the leather is cut out in the shape of a star.

When I ask Mom, "Who is Jesus?" she tells me, "He was a rabbi and a leader who was killed because of his beliefs. His killers, the Romans, called him King of the Jews. And when he was dead, he became more important."

"So dead makes you more important?"

"Well, not always," she continues. "Sometimes people make bigger stories out of death and out come new leaders—bigger than life."

I start making a mental list: Donavan at school says I killed Christ.

"Is Christ more important dead than alive, Mom?" But she doesn't answer.

And when I see Babette, I ask her, "Are Christ and Jesus the same person?"

"Yes," she says, and adds, "silly goose." I always know she loves me when she calls me special names. I call her Freckle Face, and wish the sun had kissed me that much, too. I wish that I was special and that

I didn't have that list of people I think I killed, like
Jesus and my mother. No one ever told me I didn't kill
them. They just clear their throats, hum, hum, hum,
and that tells me I'm right. That's what I hear in my
head. I did kill them. But then the same voices come
back and say, "Oh, my God, no, because how could
such a thing be true?"

"Well, if I didn't kill my mother, where is she?" I
ask my father again. "Is she in Chicago? You said she
is."

"Well, no," he replies.

"Then is she with Baby Jesus?"

"Who told you that?"

"Donavan at school."

I tell him that Donavan says that to me when he
tells me I killed Baby Jesus, every day during recess
and more often if he can. Except I run home ahead of
him, hand in hand with Babette, and we laugh. And
when he gets closer we hide behind a tree, hugging, so
we are smaller than the trunk.

She tells me she'll make me St. Jeanne because she
heard of this lady with my name who's a saint.

"But was she Jewish?" I ask her.

"No, silly."

"What happened to her?"

"My mom said she was burned at the stake because
she tried to help God."

That's not what I want to happen to me, but I try to feel the fire licking at my feet and be brave so I could just stand there and let it happen because Babette thinks she is a saint, and that's the best you can be, besides Baby Jesus.

So on my list of the dead is Alice, Baby Jesus, Bubbie, and Saint Jeanne. Do they know each other in heaven? Will I see them when I go there?

Then comes my favorite part:

"Saint Jeanne, come here," Babette shouts. She wants me to come over and see the seesaw her father made for her.

"Come here to me," she says as I come running across the street to her house. We both run to the backyard and jump on the seesaw like we do on our imaginary horses, facing each other, pushing back and forth, the friction of our shorts and the seats rubbing between our legs, the faster we go, up and down. We smile at each other in a trance. We become saints. We fly up to heaven. We glaze over and keep seesawing.

I think, *Maybe Jews do have saints after all.*

The Summer Grandma Goldenberg Got Sick

My mother's voice comes booming in the still of an August summer day. It is so loud that I hear it all the way from where she is calling by the back door of our house across the street at Babette's, where we are playing under the cover of her front porch. It doesn't sound like my mother's usual voice. It is pushed, stretched, frightened, so much so that I quickly run across the street, with Babette trailing me, through the gate and directly into the house. I know something is wrong because my mother would never let flies come in through an open door.

"It's Grandma," she says to me when she runs into the kitchen to meet me. "She doesn't look good." Grandma, who is staying with us for a while, is sitting on the couch with sweat pouring off her forehead, her hair all up like she'd just taken a shower.

"Quick," Mom says, "put on a dress. Dad is coming to get us from the store, and we're going to the doctor."

That is the day I learn my grandma has cancer as well as heart problems. I know about her heart because I overheard Mom and Dad talking about it one evening when they thought I was asleep. I didn't know exactly what they meant, but I know it is serious. I know that my father takes pills every day and he is fine. But Grandma, sitting there on the couch, is looking a little gray. I heard Mom tell Dad, "She looks ashen," when she called him back to say, "Hurry."

We get into the car when Dad pulls up. Cousin Gerald is minding the grocery store along with the butcher. They can keep an eye on everything. Gerald has a bad temper so he can't always be trusted, but this is an emergency.

It is dark when we get home after leaving Grandma at the hospital, where the doctor told us to take her. Mom and Dad say nothing, which is unusual, because my mother always has something to say. Most nights my dad just sits there nodding yes, or reads his paper, usually the sports section, and says, "Uh-huh," as my mother tells him the story of her day, or mine. But this night, silence reigns over the meal and the evening. My mom calls the hospital around 8 p.m. because they told her she could check to see how Grandma is doing. But that is the only sound, no questions, no radio shows, and no music. That night we go to bed covered in silence and wake up in the morning the same way.

I get up a little later because it is summer. Mom feeds me breakfast and then tells me, "I just spoke to Grandma's doctor. She can come home tomorrow," and that is all she says.

That night I hear my mother whimpering and my father comforting her. "At least she'll come back here tomorrow."

It's so strange to hear my mother cry. She is always strong with just about everything, Dad says, and he's proud of her for that. And then I suddenly remember and blurt out, "Don't worry." I know that my first mother has come to me and told me not to be frightened.

When we get Grandma the next day, which is Sunday, I greet her with a big kiss and a hug.

"I heard a voice," I tell her. "The voice said, 'Don't worry, don't worry.'"

And that afternoon Grandma and I sit on the couch in the living room. She is reading her book. I trace the pattern of the couch fabric, not wanting to leave her side except when I go to the bathroom or when it is time to help Mom prepare dinner, and even then, I keep an eye on Grandma through the open door that goes from the kitchen into the living room.

After I help Mom with the dinner dishes, I ask Grandma, "Are you really fine?" to which she replies, "As good as can be."

I go to bed without a worry or a care.

Life is back to normal now. Grandma plays cards with her women's group, Mom is happy and talks to Dad in the evenings, Dad nods and speaks his usual few words. Summer goes on, as it should. Nothing much changes but the pages of the calendar after Bubbie Simonoff died. Babette and I continue to play one day at my house and one day at hers. Nothing bad will ever happen again. We are spared.

1949

Today We Woke Up to Snow

This is January 1949, on the day we wake up to snow. In Southern California, weather doesn't change more than a few degrees and the last leaf usually falls off the tree in sheer exhaustion around Thanksgiving, for the tree only to begin budding again the next week.

My mother brings out the Brownie box camera because this is a special occasion for a picture, like my birthday parties, or holding my violin, or with my first cowgirl outfit, or on my new bike with my Uncle Itzy when he came back from the service.

January is the time of the camellias, the time of predictable weather—down to the fifties and cold at night—but this morning we awoke to snow.

Mom says to me, "Get on your powder-blue wool coat and your mittens."

"Can I go across the street and get Babette?"

"Yes, I'll get the camera," Mom says.

Dad is going off to work bundled in his tan khaki pants, his heavy wool socks and work shoes, and a big wool sweater. He hesitates and waves as I come running back across the street with Babette, who is in a plaid coat with a hood, the red in the plaid darker than her flaming hair. We both have grins on our faces as we jump up and down and lean over to make snowballs like I saw in a movie with Lana Turner and Gary Cooper, or was it Rhonda Fleming and Gary Cooper? Just like Gary made a snowball and threw it at Rhonda or Lana, I throw a snowball at Babette. Babette, startled, stares at me in surprise, and then she laughs and throws one back. Dad stands there with his hands on his hips as my next snowball gets him right in his face. Babette and I each have a snowball in our hands, ready to throw them, when Mom, looking through the camera, says, "Stop. Smile."

We freeze in ecstasy.

I don't remember whether we go to school or not because this is a holiday, a special day, a day when friends play with each other in total joy and abandonment as if nothing else matters and this time will go on forever.

We have hot chocolate and cookies followed by giggling, and we rush back out to try to make a snowman before the sun comes out. We get a small one made, although it leaves most of the green lawn exposed. But we know it has been a miracle, the beginning of a new year, a special and joyous year. And then as quickly as the snow comes and goes, so do Babette and her family.

One day she is across the street, the next day we are saying goodbye and exchanging special words, like "best friends." And I give her my favorite rock, bird feathers from the blackbirds that made a nest in the large tree in my backyard, cat's eye marbles, and a special lariat I made that past summer at camp. Babette gives me a little cross. She calls it a crucifix, and my mother says that it is a special thing for Babette, and makes me give it back.

That Saturday the moving truck pulls up in front of the Boyers' house. The movers begin dismantling our life, Babette's and mine. First her living room with the overstuffed couch and its forest-green chenille upholstery, then the rust-colored armchair, the bentwood rocker, the small RCA television, and the next thing I know, Babette is getting into the back of her parents' 1940 beige Ford and waving as they drive away forever.

The Holiday Story

It's a school holiday. I'm happy I don't have to walk a long way to school and face Donavan, especially since Babette is gone. I wonder where she is now, months after she rode off with her parents, who packed up their house right after New Year's. It seems like she's been gone for so long. Here it is, the day after Easter Sunday, and it was only last year that Babette and her family went to the Hollywood Bowl for Easter sunrise services.

On the first day of Easter vacation there's an article on the front page of the *Los Angeles Times* about these sunrise services, and a second article on another page. My father reads this and calls out, "Honey, come here." Mom takes off the rubber gloves she wears to do the dishes. I set the dishtowel on the countertop next to her gloves, and run over. Dad says, "Look, right here in the *Los Angeles Times*, on the back page in part one. 'JEWS FORGIVEN. They did not kill Christ,' and right next to it, a picture of the pope."

Mom says, "Now, isn't that just wonderful," only she doesn't sound like she's happy, but more like when she expects me to clean up my room, and she comes in and says, "Well," as she runs her finger along my dresser, "isn't that just wonderful," and blows the dust off.

But I want to celebrate like we do on New Year's Day with the Rose Parade with me sitting tall upon a beautiful horse—like the one Dale Evans rides—and dressed in a royal purple robe like Queen Esther.

I want to ride my horse right up to Donavan's house and make someone go up and knock on his front door, and when his mom opens it, I'll say, "Bring out your son, Donavan." And when he comes out onto the porch, right there is a banner strung all across the street, "INNOCENT—JEWS INNOCENT. They didn't do it."

"Do what?" he'll say.

"Kill Christ. You did," and I will point to Donavan, who looks up stunned and says, "I didn't." Then I'll shout back at Donavan, as everyone looks up at the Queen of the Parade, who is me: "Neither did I!"

Donavan's Hollering

I

Each time I hear his voice hollering to me, I think of the people in the Nazi concentration camps during World War II, guards screaming at mothers, fathers, and children to go here and do that. The victims are the ones in the photographs in *LIFE Magazine*, the ones the Nazi guards rounded up and took away to the death camps.

Donavan's voice burns through my every thought, accusing me of a treacherous act. Like a hunter tracking me down for the kill, he hollers out, "You killed Christ. You must die." And in some way a small piece of me does, or goes underground to hide, fears gathering under a cloak of dread. I try to free myself, but there is no let-up. Day after day his voice is present. Day after day on my way to and from school, I brace myself against his attacks and wonder why he chooses to persecute me. I think, *Why not Lupe next door?* After all, she's different. Her parents are from Mexico. They speak Spanish at home. I think of my grandparents, who came by ship into another harbor in the early 1900s and were greeted by the lady with the torch that I had seen in my history book. And yet, right here in Eagle Rock, I am not free. Not that I'm tied up in chains like the Africans who we also saw in photographs, or the Indians who became slaves to the missionaries because they were told their lives would be better if they believed in the Catholic religion. But this small boy my own age that reigns terror on me because my religion is Judaism, and because he must have been told I was responsible for the brutal slaughter of the son of God. I know this is a form of slavery that ties me to him, puts me at his mercy, day after day, unable to escape. There is no Moses to lead me out of the land this child holds me captive in.

"Mom, why does he do this to me?" I ask, crying so hard it feels like I will never stop. And she tells me, "You must be strong. He's just an ignorant young boy who has his story all mixed up."

"But can't someone tell him the right story?" I beg. "I don't even want to go to school because every day he follows me."

"You must be brave," my mother says. "Our people have been forced to be brave and even die for our beliefs. After all, we are the chosen people," Mom says.

"Who chose us?"

"God."

"Did God know Donavan would do this to me?"

"God doesn't watch every small thing."

"But, Mom, isn't this an injustice?"

I say this because my third-grade teacher told us that slavery was an injustice. "Then isn't 'dirty Jew' the same thing?"

"Be strong," is all she says.

"Was it like this when you were a child?"

"No, it wasn't. Not in St. Paul."

"Could we just go live there then?"

Later that night, I overhear my mother telling my father what has happened. My father says in response, "Well, we just can't pick up and move."

So that next day and every day after that I put on my coat of armor and my mother's blessing and set out on a path that is laced with terror and grief.

II

Mom taught me I could step in and stand up, even in the worst times. Even though Donavan screamed at me every day on the way to school. He showed no mercy. I didn't see Donavan on weekends, holidays, and summers. But I was still afraid. His cry, "You killed Christ," rings in my ears and remains with me.

I've decided I won't let him torture me.

My new mission: to bring Donavan out into the open.

I walk to school; the day is warm. It is September right before Rosh Hashanah. My hands are sweaty.

I hear Donavan behind me a block back then his footsteps come closer, louder and louder. Then the words, as if he's breathing down my neck. I can't feel his words, though they come with the moisture of the day. He is down by Mrs. White's house. I am two houses up, almost to the next corner where we turn and head toward school.

The words fan out in the heat of summer. Donavan shouts his chant. I can feel my stomach knotting, my pulse racing, trapped in a dream that is a waking nightmare. The words pour out towards me. "You dirty Jew girl, you..." and then I stop listening. I start to pray for him—to pretend that it is already Yom Kippur. That we are in temple when we come to the list of God's decisions once and for all about who shall live and who shall die by fire. Who by drowning. And I imagine Donavan falling into a deep hole in the bottom of the Eagle Rock Swimming Pool and no matter how hard I pray for him, God's wrath pulls him down under. It's the same place where I almost drowned but came up for help screaming, sounds muffled in water and then loud into air.

In my imagination Donavan is drowning, screaming for help, but no one comes to his rescue. All his sounds stay under. None of the screams reach the air or the light or the hot day. And then peace comes over me.

I realize I am running so fast that I leave Donavan almost a block back, the words silenced by the distance. I have escaped him this time. It is just as I felt when I woke up the day after Yom Kippur and was still alive. God has indeed spared me. When I get to school safely, I don't think about the walk home or the day. All I know is I am saved. And the very best part of it is that I learn, for the moment, how to save myself.

1950

A Mother's Worry

"She'll be safer that way," I hear my father say.

I ask Mom, "Safer from what?"

"Oh, nothing," she replies. But I know Mom believes the stories about Donavan and she begins walking to school with me.

"Good exercise," she tells me, but I know she's worried.

When my dad gets home at night, she greets him with the usual hug and kiss and I do, too.

"No incidents," is all she says.

"Good."

Mom walks me almost all the way to school, but not quite, because I tell her that after the first week my friend Marilyn Morgan, who lives right across the street from school, and her friend Beverly, who lives up the block from her, said, "That's funny," because no one else has their mother come with them except the babies, by which they meant the kindergarteners and first-graders. Even some of them walk to school by themselves.

Marilyn wants to know, "Why does she do that?"

I have to tell her about Donavan, and that, two weeks before, he burned a cross in our front lawn that I saw with my own eyes. "I was sitting on the couch, and when I heard a noise, I looked out the front window. There was Donavan. He was pouring something in the shape of a large X, and then lit a match to it so it went up in flames. I couldn't believe my eyes. I went outside and I smelled the grass where it burned."

Marilyn thinks it's some kind of prank. She doesn't really understand how much I suffer. I want to go to his father and tell him, "Stop all this," say something to him about the cross and the fact that his son continues to bother me almost daily.

"Why would he burn a cross?" Marilyn asks.

"Because I'm Jewish."

"But I know that and I don't burn a cross on your lawn."

"You don't yell at me on the way to school and on the way home like he does, either."

"You mean like when he says…"

"Yes, that I killed Christ."

"Well, I know you didn't. Christ died years ago for all of our sins, so how could you have killed him?"

"I wish I knew more about that."

"I can tell you as much as you want," she says.

"Well, maybe later," I say and I see my mother walking up the street.

"Sometime you'll have to stay and play at my house," Marilyn says.

"I have to ask my mom," and thank her for the invitation.

"Wait until you're a little older," my mother says. But my mother knows best, so I never bring it up again.

My mom is scared. She wants to protect me. She tells me, "In a world such as ours, after we fought to stop Hitler and the killing of the Jews, I never felt as safe as I did when I was a small girl, able to walk home by myself, in my Jewish neighborhood of St. Paul, Minnesota, unharmed. The war put an end to all that."

1951

Working with My Father

During the summer, Dad invites me to go to his grocery store with him.

"Get ready, we leave at eight o'clock and we have a lot of work to do," he says to me.

We get into my dad's 1937 dull green Chevy. We drive past the street where Bubbie and Zadie lived before Bubbie died and now are pulling up to the corner where a big sign across the top front of the building says Simonoff's Friendly Market. I can feel the excitement in anticipation of what Zaydie taught me about working with him in his small grocery stand.

The first thing visible is the fruits and vegetables: the nectarines beginning to blush as they become redder and redder; the carrots, with their lacey green tops; the beets, both red and yellow. The apples and oranges, the tangerines and grapes. The apples, with their different tones of yellows and reds, are polished with a rag, so shiny you can almost see the sky in them.

Although my father went to school to become a teacher, I can see his love of his store.

"Dad, where should I start?"

"Start with the apples. They need the most work."

I pick up an apple as my father hands me a small, dry, cloth towel.

"Like this," he reminds me, as he takes a red, dull apple and polishes it with his towel until the light film is removed.

"Dad, like this?" I say as I hand him my first completed work.

"What do you see?"

"Me," I say. "Me."

"That's it. Now continue."

Once I finish that job, I know the next thing is to dust the canned goods with a feather duster that my father always puts in his back right pocket. After two hours of arranging and polishing, I go to the stockroom to begin dusting back stock.

My father prides himself on having fair prices and owns the only grocery store in the neighborhood that extends credit to his customers in between their paydays. Sometimes after we close the store, my father grabs a couple of bags of groceries and hands one to me. "To take to the shut-ins," he tells me, and I never do see him get any money for these.

When I say something to Mom, she asks him if he got paid. He stands there as she shakes her head. "Not again," is all she says.

Throughout the days that follow, I continue to check with my father after each task is completed. There is never a hug or a kiss, just a smile across his face that says it all.

"I love you, Dad," I say one day, as we drive home after a full day's work.

"What makes you say that?"

"I don't know. I just do." He doesn't need to say anything. I have what I have been missing.

The summer continued that way and the next summer after that.

Those were the best times I had with my father.

Then Safeway came into the neighborhood. My father's customers began to go over there to save a penny or two. He had to close down his store and take a job as a food salesman. He was never quite the same after that, and neither were my mom and I.

1952

Grandma Goldenberg

A few years have passed since Grandma got sick. Mom and I go over to her apartment and play hearts, which she taught me.

At the end of the summer, Mom and Dad take Grandma back to the hospital and give Lupe instructions to answer the telephone if it rings.

Our house seems too quiet. No radio playing. No one telling me to wash my face and ears or brush my teeth. Only me and Lupe from next door, who sits on the couch reading from a *Photoplay Magazine*.

We were looking at the pictures of Marilyn Monroe in a new magazine. "Hot off the newsstand," Lupe says to me and smiles, as she puts her arm around me to pull me close to her.

Lupe's house is along the fence line near the cemetery for all the turtles, and close to the incinerator.

She tells me about her and Marilyn Monroe and that some day she'll bleach her hair blonde just like her. I laugh because she has long, wavy black hair and dark brown eyes and is not light-skinned like Marilyn. We both laugh. "Imagine, you with blonde hair. That's funny," I say, and she answers right back, "Well, you never know until you try it."

We continue to flip through the magazine, stopping once in a while for her to tell me how much she loves some actor who has dark hair like her and is very handsome. Rock Hudson.

"He's new," she says and explains that he just became a movie star and reminds her of her boyfriend, Salvador, who joined the navy so he can get an education when he gets out. "Otherwise," she tells me, "his family said he can't go to college."

College is what I want to do when I grow up, I tell her, because my father went to college and my mother didn't and she says I will go when I'm ready."

Then it is time for some peanut butter cookies my mom baked this morning and left on a plate on the stove. Just as Lupe is bringing them over and goes back to get the glasses of milk, the phone rings. She answers it.

"Yes, Mrs. Simonoff, I'll tell her." When she hangs up, she looks very pale. "Your parents will be home by dinnertime."

"What about Grandma?" I ask her, even though I know Grandma will never be coming back.

"They'll tell you when they get home."

"Let's pick some flowers from the backyard for Mom. She'll be very sad."

Remembering

November is the tail end of summer in Los Angeles. There is heaviness in the air. We have all the mirrors covered, because in Jewish law, when someone dies and you are in mourning, you don't look at your reflection.

It's not like I think it will be. Mom sits there shaking her head, "She's gone."

I'm back in school and when I get home, I check in with my mom, get my book, and sit down next to her. She wants to go over to her sister's, Aunt Minnie's, but she doesn't drive and the bus ride would only put us at Eagle Rock Boulevard, which means we would still have a long way to walk to Aunt Minnie's house. By that time it would be getting too dark.

When I get home the next day, there's Aunt Minnie and Joey.

"Where's Mike?" Mike is Joey's older brother.

"He's over at Brubsey's," who is Gary Craigmire, Mike's best friend, Aunt Minnie tells me. It seems Aunt Minnie told him to go there when class was over. She takes Joey, Mike's younger sister, out of school early so Joey can come over and play with me while Aunt Minnie visits with Mom.

Joey and I go to the back of the living room to play behind the couch and Aunt Minnie and Mom sit around crying and laughing and talking, a photograph album sitting on their laps.

"Remember that one, when Mama first met Papa?"

"In Russia."

First there are Grandma's children, Uncle Max and Uncle Jules, and my mother. Then, a short time later, come Aunt Minnie and Uncle Itzy. There's even a picture of Grandpa Goldenberg standing with Grandma and the children taken when they first got to St. Paul. Then there are all the photographs that have accumulated of her life here in Los Angeles, with her children, save Uncle Itzy, who was still a medic in World War II. Then photos of Aunt Minnie and Uncle Gordon and then of Mike as a baby, followed in three years by Joey. There are photos of the old times: Mom, young, with her group of women friends, at the lake on holiday; or Mom with one of her boyfriends down at the beach near St. Paul, before she met Dad. Aunt Minnie calls the man in the photograph Herman the Vermin, because he is what she calls "underhanded," and because he also smokes cigars. Sometimes I looked at these albums with Mom but it would be fun to look at them with Joey and Aunt Minnie.

Joey and I decide to sit next to Mom and Aunt Minnie so we can all look at the pictures together. Joey brings over my doll, Susie, who still sits on my bed. She has been having a conversation with her about how sad her mother is.

When Mom and Aunt Minnie see us, they set the photograph album down on the coffee table in front of them. I wedge in next to my mother and Joey jumps up onto her mother's lap. Both of them wrap their arms around us.

I laugh because Joey sits on Aunt Minnie's lap and Susie on Joey's.

"Look at you two," Mom says, and I add, "You three." Then we all laugh, a sound that is welcomed in our house of mourning.

By spring I leave early in the morning to walk to junior high school, because I am in the orchestra, and must warm up before class. I carry my violin case to the orchestra room. My fingers are cold as I place them on the strings at 8:30 a.m.

My violin sends out sounds into the open air I never thought I could make. I begin to play songs. Ruby, Frenesi, some gypsy airs. The violin is my best friend.

Mom seems to be getting over Grandma's death, although I know that the summer will be hard because the two of us will be listening to soap operas without Grandma. I know she and Aunt Minnie will be on the phone after each fifteen-minute episode, telling each other what they think should have happened.

When I come home from school Mom gives me an update on *Ma Perkins* and *Our Gal Sunday*, who came from a mining town in the west hoping to find wealth and happiness with Lord Henry Brinthrip. Mom's favorite is *The Romance of Helen Trent*. I can't remember much about Helen but Mom fills me in on the episode of the day as I used to hear her do with Grandma. I sit patiently, although I really want to go to my room and practice, and just then my mom tells me she has gotten me a music stand, and that I can actually practice in the living room now.

I know that she wants the company and I try to imagine what it would be like without my mother. I know that feeling, being without a mother, but that was so long ago, I can hardly remember it now.

I don't mention Grandma much because I know it will make Mom sad and, one day after I finish practicing, she says, "You know, you can talk about Grandma if you want."

"I thought it would make you sad," is all I say, and start talking about Grandma more.

On Friday nights at services, Mom and Aunt Minnie and sometimes Uncle Itzy stand near the end of the services to say the special prayer for the dead in honor of Grandma. I remember some of the words. "*Yisgadal veyiskadash*," and then they cry but continue with the prayer.

Sometimes I play a song for Grandma when I'm alone, one that I made up, because I know that wherever she is, she can hear it loud, then soft, music that my mother tells me sounds like the Yiddish songs she grew up with and I know Grandma hears the same thing, as I hold her here in my heart.

The mirrors in the house were uncovered after one week and Grandma's clothes were given away to charity. Her candlesticks are still lit on Friday nights to welcome in the *Shabbas* Queen. I hear Grandma saying the blessing. Some things are never forgotten.

The Last Straw

I'm eleven. I've been reading Hebrew for the last three years. I'm getting ready to be bas mitzvahed. I practice hard every day. I memorize all the blessings. My voice rings straight to God. I know it. My body tells me. I have feelings that don't have words. I hold them for a long time, as long as I can remember. If something is true, I know; if it is not, I know that, too.

I have trouble on one part of my portion of *Haftorah,* something from the Prophets. They're the stories created when Jews were forbidden to read Torah. Stories taught the lessons.

There is no music to sing with the stories, just symbols that represent various musical notes. Sometimes I go home and play the melody on my violin as I remember it. The sounds of the notes imprint on my brain and call themselves back. Regular school and Hebrew school go on as usual.

It's early in June and a few degrees warmer in Highland Park, where the temple is because it's further inland. When it's the end of the school year, we won't go to Hebrew school in the afternoon on Tuesdays and Thursdays after regular school.

The rabbi walks toward us. "I have something to tell all of you," he starts out. "I received an offer to be a rabbi at a big temple in the east. I will be leaving but I will remember each and every one of you."

I hear my name being called out. "Jeanne, what is the beginning of the prayer for the blessing before...?"

"Now, all of you who are preparing for your bar mitzvah," the rabbi continues, "will be given a special tutor who will continue to get you ready. You will begin where we left off. It will be as if I am still here. Just like I'm still here with you. You are good students."

All I can think of is what he said, "bar mitzvah." Not bas mitzvah. I've been cut out. Will I ever take my rightful place?

It feels like it is over; all my plans for my bas mitzvah, gone. A bas mitzvah is something no girls have asked for in my synagogue, but I have taken it seriously and know that for me, somehow, it will be different and it will happen. But when the rabbi speaks, inside I feel myself scream and that scream fills up my head. Although I just sit there, I see myself running out the door, out to the center of the street on Monte Vista, hollering, "I can't have this happen." Not a muscle in my body moves. I'm here but not here. I remember all that I need to know for my ceremony but put it all away.

The vision continues. I don't want the streetcars and automobiles to stop; I want to be hit by a car and die real fast. Then they'll take me to the cemetery in a box like the pine one with no nails in the Orthodox way, like Bubbie was buried. My family and friends, as well as the rabbi, will come and cry. I will be up there in heaven with a woman who looks familiar and knows my name. She will comfort me and tell me she understands. But I know no one really does. Again I've lost what I loved and wanted. I want to be the same as my cousins. The same as the boys. This loss is of an eight magnitude on the Richter scale, causing whole cities to fall into the sea, people drowning in an ocean of fear and abandonment.

I am deep into this reverie when the rabbi asks me the question, "What is the beginning word of the Torah blessing?" I just stare at him. I can still feel it, the deep hollow ache with no words. All I want to do is die, or be held.

I hear the rabbi's voice telling all of us, "You can get the name of your tutor after school. Or better yet, I will call your parents and give them all the information. Now let's continue. Let's go on." I begin to doubt everything. I wonder if my parents will let my bas mitzvah even happen.

"Jeanne, I asked you what is the beginning of the *brucha*. If you need help, just ask for it. I'm here to help you. I am here to teach you. I am here. Jeanne, do you hear me?"

I say the blessing. I don't see what difference it makes. I feel flat and dead. I am beginning the motions of a girl who is gone. *"Barechu et Adonai hamevorah..."* I continue. I am here. I am not here. The rabbi comes toward me. His face looks like he is ready to ask me a question.

"Jeanne, what's the matter?" he asks. "You don't sound like yourself. Where are you? Where did you go? Didn't you study? You told me you were ready. Jeanne, Jeanne!" He is right in my face but I make him a ghost.

"I must begin to prepare myself," I tell him. He has not done his job.

"Jeanne?" he reaches out and touches my shoulder. I feel him there.

"Are you here?"

"Yes."

"Didn't you study?"

"Yes, of course I studied. But I didn't think you would ever leave me."

"Leave you? Jeanne, I am leaving but someone else will take my place. I will let your parents know," he says to reassure me.

I hear the words. They echo through me. They go down into a cave. They wait for a sign. They try to reform what there was before this announcement. I see myself on the *bimah,* the pulpit. I hear myself start. I see myself stop. Then, the rabbi and my parents take me off. They remove me. They take off my *tallis*, my prayer shawl. They roll up the Torah scrolls.

They place the Torah back into the ark. Then there is darkness.

The days that follow are meaningless. I can only wait to see if what I am afraid of happening will really happen.

My mother and father tell me they got a call from the rabbi. I can be confirmed, they tell me, and that is just as good as bas mitzvah. I tell them, "No, I want to be the one by myself up on the *bimah* saying the prayers and touching the sacred scrolls, following all the words in my portion of the week, becoming a woman, like my cousins Mike, Martin, and David will become men with their bar mitzvah."

But they still don't understand how important it is to me. "Please let me do it," I beg them, but it is no use. It feels like God himself has abandoned me.

The following week begins summer vacation with all the daytime soap operas: *The Romance of Helen Trent*, *Our Gal Sunday*, and *Ma Perkins*. Mom and I sit by the radio each morning. We listen to all of these. I can't sit still too long before I want to go and play. With no Hebrew school and no bas mitzvah, everything else has no meaning.

I retreat from my religion but go through all the rituals—Friday night services after the ushering in of the *Shabbas* Queen, with lighting the candles and the prayer over the wine. Then we go to temple for services.

I'm eleven years old. It's the summer of 1952, the year of remorse and broken vows. I can't remember much else.

When my friends left me, I believed. When Donavan told me I killed Christ, I believed. When I couldn't be bas mitzvahed, I believed in something but lost my way. When everything I believed in failed, I believed anyway as children do.

A child doesn't understand the finality of death. My mother went to Chicago on holiday. I waited and searched for her. She never returned. The silence of the death is real, genuine, literal and true. A part of me would grieve for the rest of my life.

I searched for Babette and couldn't find her.

Donavan receded into the background, too. Maybe he moved. But he no longer held me captive. My school life went forward. I matured and my world opened up. I developed a relationship, one of love. Friends who gathered around me respected who I was: a blues singer who sang Motherless Child, a guitar player, poet, Jewish lesbian with strong roots in my culture. I had a belief in something that covered me through all those years as a counselor. My longitude and latitude was set. Still a chord needed to be drawn back. The music became loud. I had to respond.

There were child sounds: rustling jasmine, wind in the trees, Zaydie clearing his throat, big Red purring, lullabies my mother must have sung. Bubbie's Russian songs as she retreated back to childhood. Lost threads and chords resounded on my violin. I heard the refrain of the minor key.

In the symphony of my life, those common chords came out. I didn't hear the melancholy of my heritage until the Saturday of my cousin Lizzie's bat mitzvah on the shores of south Lake Tahoe. She stood before her congregation, with a temporary ark that held the torah placed on a table, in a country club that may have denied membership to Jews in the fifties and sixties. There she chanted her *maftir*, her torah portion.

I felt my chords become harmonious, reaching to send me out into the world to take my place and become whole.

The sorrow of Alice, the hatred of Donavan, the lightness of Babette receded. Underneath that, the years have flown by. I don't see Donavan or Babette, but they've left an indelible impression on me now that I'm a grown woman. It is the fragility of a spirit, of first love, and friendship. My music, my beliefs and ceremony now have voice.

Epilogue—2002

Mother, I look for your remains inside walls and crypts, caged behind a two-inch slab faced with your name.

I bring flowers, gather water for the vases no longer there, and search for these down the row, dusty rings that held them, vases dusty, memories all dust in the burial chamber.

Can I exhume more than isolated facts and recreate a whole from decomposed matter? You're a handful of dust I can't mix with memory and make whole.

What do I expect, some part of the sky to crack open and hand you to me, creating a facsimile when even your books— Moliere, The Count of Monte Cristo, *in French— mold, fade, or just plain disappear?*

What I have now are musty smells only books hold, something about the air the morning you died, my memory of you before words, as I lay in my crib, covers binding, trying to claw my way out and run to you when you called me.

I hear you, without voice, utter, "It's too bad I couldn't leave a note like a suicide. But I will sneak these last bits of me between pages of my favorite books. Scatter hints around the country so you will not walk into places a stranger.

"It's a puzzle. Place all the pieces out in front of you. Memories of me. How my smile looked. Picture of my hand holding your hand.

"Think of it, Jeanne, as a scavenger hunt, with these fragments a map, a language that mirrors early morning, some sand left in your eyes."

I am called to the Torah. The voice that comes out of my throat is that of a young tenor. It is a child of eight, who begins study. It is her soul. She wants to become part of a large community she pulls to her as family. She studies very hard and remembers the words her adoptive mother tells her, words she was given as a gift from her father. "Kinder, there is only one thing that they can't take away from you and that, my dear one, is knowledge."

In 2001, I decided to pick up what I had left behind, ready to fill in the gap where my faith was ripped out, convinced that I could relearn the Hebrew I had studied so hard long ago. At age sixty-one, I began my journey to bat mitzvah.

After twelve long months of study, I learned my Torah portion, first with vowels, then with melody, chanting the same sounds as the ancient rabbis who came before. I followed the words written on parchment with the yad, a silver pointer.

But I am worried if I can lift the Torah, this tree of knowledge, and carry its fifty-pound weight. Would my body let me down? Would my broken shoulders bear its weight as I had borne the sadness and loss of being denied my rite, the chance to stand up in front of my peers and be called to the Torah? Could I bring it down off its high place in the Holy Ark, and carry it all around the congregation? And would my mother, with her failing heart and mind, understand that I have taken my place as a daughter of the commandments?

My mother was called to the Torah at the age of seventy-five. Tears filled my eyes as she read her portion, her *Haftorah*, in a strong, steady voice. Her faith never wavered. I wish I had asked her what prompted her to do it. As the daughter of an Orthodox rabbi who came over from Russia to freely practice his Judaism, she watched him carry his *tallit* bag to temple on Shabbat and read Torah, shepherding small boys not yet thirteen to enter their place in the congregation. I wonder if she resented the inequality of women within that sacred passage, how they had to sit, out of sight, in the balcony while the men, including her three brothers, came forward and read their portion of the Torah.

Words spread out across my memory exactly as it looked on the formidable parchment stitched together. Letters marching right to left, words attempting escape from my mouth, dry as the summer rocks.

I wanted it all to pour down on me, cleanse me, and render me whole.

My mother sits in the front row as I take my place at the *bimah*, where we stand to read the Torah. Her eyes tell me she is fading in and out. Alzheimer's has claimed much of our past together. Suddenly, she snaps into the present as I am given my father's *tallit*, and hollers out in a loud voice, "That's my daughter!"

Tears wash over me as the congregation begins the *Shehecheyanu* blessing, said when one does something for the very first time. With my *tallit* wrapped around me, I stand and sing with them, thanking God for sustaining us and bringing us to this day. Here I am. I move forward to my final destination and bring myself. It is fifty years later.

I lead the congregation in prayer. I take the Torah out from the Ark, as I have practiced during these past few weeks, and there I stand, the weight of it distributed against the top of my right shoulder and across my heart, balanced by my hands clutching the two scrolls. I hear my mother's voice say, "Safe, be safe. Don't falter." This weight is not too much to bear.

I take the Torah down to the congregation, marching up the center aisle as people lean over and touch their prayer book or the corner of their *tallit* to the Torah and then to their lips. It is all of ours, this tree of life, this Torah. I pass my family, who has come to bear witness to my passage. I return to the *bimah*.

Borochu et Adonai Hamevorach. Blessed is the One to whom our praise is due. The congregation replies, *Baruch Adonai hamevorach leolam vaed*! Blessed be the One to whom our praise is due, now and forever! I repeat this sentence and continue the call and response. I have been invited into Torah. I reach that place of remembrance, and, yes, that place of forgiveness and redemption.

I now know this miracle: I have returned home, whole. Let all who wish to stand here with me and be blessed, rise.

I am called to the Torah.